40 days of Surrender

40 days of Surrender

Jeanette M. Towne

© 2021 by Jeanette M. Towne. All rights reserved.

Published by Redemption Press, PO Box 427, Enumclaw, WA 98022.
Toll-Free (844) 2REDEEM (273-3336)

Redemption Press is honored to present this title in partnership with the author. The views expressed or implied in this work are those of the author. Redemption Press provides our imprint seal representing design excellence, creative content, and high-quality production.

The author has tried to recreate events, locales, and conversations from memories of them. In order to maintain their anonymity, in some instances the names of individuals, some identifying characteristics, and some details may have been changed, such as physical properties, occupations, and places of residence.

Noncommercial interests may reproduce portions of this book without the express written permission of the author, provided the text does not exceed five hundred words. When reproducing text from this book, include the following credit line: "40 Days of Surrender by Jeanette M. Towne. Used by permission."

Commercial interests: No part of this publication may be reproduced in any form, stored in a retrieval system, or transmitted in any form by any means—electronic, photocopy, recording, or otherwise—without prior written permission of the publisher/author, except as provided by United States of America copyright law.

Unless otherwise indicated, all Scripture quotations are from the Holy Bible, New International Version®, NIV®. Copyright © 1973, 1978, 1984, 2011 by Biblica, Inc.™ Used by permission of Zondervan. All rights reserved worldwide. www.zondervan.com The "NIV" and "New International Version" are trademarks registered in the United States Patent and Trademark Office by Biblica, Inc.™

Scripture quotations marked (NLT) are taken from the Holy Bible, New Living Translation, copyright ©1996, 2004, 2015 by Tyndale House Foundation. Used by permission of Tyndale House Publishers, Carol Stream, Illinois 60188. All rights reserved.

ISBN 13: 978-1-68314-968-2 (Paperback)
978-1-68314-969-9 (ePub)
978-1-68314-970-5 (Mobi)

Library of Congress Catalog Card Number: 2021918929

The Hand of God

The heart of my faith is cradled in the One who holds my hand.
He created me and has known me since before time began.
When I was born, He gave me breath and ordained that I would stand
Within the sea of humanity, though merely a grain of sand.
When I contemplate His majesty and the mystery of His plan,
I get lost within the magnitude of the great, Almighty I AM.
For who am I that He should lead me by His sovereign hand?
And why would He desire the love of this lowly, sinful man?

Yet, I can't deny my need for Him as I stumble along life's road.
For alone I lose my foothold and bemoan my puny load.
I'm weak and without stamina, fearful I might implode,
But I never do because God's hand I oh so tightly hold.
I'm grateful when I've wandered that He's restored me to the fold.
And grown my trust and faith, still teaching me as I grow old.
He's engraved my name upon His hand as His true word has told.
Forever I will grip His hand—more precious to me than gold.

~ Shirlee Abbington

Table of Contents

The Study Group: Eleven Courageous Women and
Their Stories 9

The Story Behind the 40 Days 11

How to Use This Study 15

The Heart of Your Faith – Days 1–4 19

My Inner Thirteen-Year-Old – Days 5–8 29

Lord, My Child Belongs to You – Days 9–12 39

My BFF – Days 13–16 45

Doing It All for God? – Days 17–20 55

Bumps in the Road to Purpose – Days 21–24 63

Credit Cards, Cash, and My ATM – Days 25–28 71

Not My Fault – Days 29–32 81

Me and My Plate – Days 33–36 89

It's My Signature Sin – Days 37–40 101

Conclusion: Celebrating the Journey 111

About the Author 113

The Study Group

Eleven Courageous Women and Their Stories

The experience that inspired *40 Days of Surrender* changed me forever, so much so that I immediately wanted to pass what I'd learned on to other women and write a book. But admittedly, when I wrote the first draft, I was the only person who had gone through the process of focused prayer and fasting that I was recommending. Would this plan resonate with others in the same way that it did me? Had I included stories that the average woman could relate to? How would women with different life experiences and faith journeys respond to my topics and challenges? What would they identify as they prayed and invited God to search their hearts?

The answers to these questions came when my publisher assigned me to a coach, who encouraged me to take a group of women through *40 Days of Surrender* and draw from their experiences and perspectives. After praying about this idea, I reached out to my home church and launched a small group for women who wanted to embrace the challenge of surrender with me. I had no idea what the response would be when I put an announcement in the bulletin.

This was most definitely a good move. Eleven women committed to the study. I ended up forming a tight bond with them as we went through *40 Days of Surrender* together and shared our experiences along the way. As I read their stories and interacted with them, I saw how uniquely and tenderly God worked in each of their lives.

Throughout this book, in addition to drawing from my own experiences, I will share highlights of the stories they shared. These women come from different backgrounds and stages of faith, but each one experienced victory and healing as they learned to surrender to God. My deepest and most sincere gratitude goes out to them for their openness and courage, both in sharing this journey of surrender with me and their willingness to open up through their written stories. Though their names have been changed to protect their privacy, I consider them valuable contributors to this book. The depth and insight they offered are priceless. Their words remind me that God has each of us on a unique path and knows exactly how to draw us in and mold us.

As you begin your own forty-day surrender journey, I pray that you will see God at work in profound ways. I encourage you to take note of what He brings to mind and the changes that take place in your heart. If you've never kept a journal before, this would be a great time to start. After experiencing the power of going through my own study with a group, I highly recommend reading this book with a friend, accountability partner, or small group, so you can share what you're learning, pray for each other, encourage each other when God reveals difficult truths, and celebrate the victories that lead to freedom and change.

May each of the next forty days bring you a little closer to the Lord, and may you see the beautiful things that happen when you surrender.

The Story behind the 40 Days

The more I get to know the Lord, the more humbled I am by the example He set while walking this earth. After being baptized, for example, Jesus went out to the desert and fasted for forty days. All God and all man, He resisted temptation and surrendered to the Father's will. In fact, His entire life illustrates surrender, from the moment He was born as a helpless infant to His torturous death on the cross. But His example in the wilderness touches me in a special way. It teaches us the importance of taking time for praying, fasting, and identifying our greatest temptations so we can have victory over them.

I thought about Jesus and His time in the wilderness often while writing this book. My passion to write *40 Days of Surrender* started where most of my ideas are birthed: while sweating and out of breath, laboring atop my cross trainer, as I worked to fight a losing battle of age, gravity, and the jello factor. I was listening to my audio Bible app and started praying. The longer I prayed, the more earnest and deep my cries to God became. I had been a believer for a long time, but that day, I wanted to do more than believe. I wanted to know God more.

I knew there were areas of my life that held me back from intimacy with Him—issues I repeatedly struggled with. The most obvious was my stubborn need for control. It tripped me up constantly. "Let go and let God," right? Yeah, bumper stickers and plaques make it sound so easy. For me, letting go is a perpetual battle.

In that tear-filled, emotional moment, I implored Him to reveal what needed to change in order for me to enjoy the closeness with Him that I craved.

Then I realized something: In Ezekiel 36:26–27, God promised to draw His people in. He told them, "I will give you a new heart and put a new spirit in you; I will remove from you your heart of stone and give you a heart of flesh. And I will put my Spirit in you and move you to follow my decrees and be careful to keep my laws."

Jeremiah 29:13 reminded me, "You will seek me and find me when you seek me with all your heart."

These words came from the same God who delivered His people from bondage. The same God who rose from the dead to save us and offer us eternal life. I was asking Him for the exact thing He wanted for each of His children: intimacy.

But I also knew that intimacy came with some requirements: a call to obedience, sacrifice, and turning away from sin. A call to seek and follow Him even when it was hard. God called His people, and even His own Son, to surrender.

Knowing Him more meant making Him my Lord. It meant giving Him everything.

I pondered what it meant to have God be my Lord, to give it all to Him. I thought of those early Israelites and felt a lot like them—stubborn, flip-flopping, changing daily and seasonally in my walk depending on my circumstances and mood. As I reflected, I saw visions of Christians who seemed to have arrived. I berated myself over the realization that I repeated the same habitual sins and controlling behavior year after year. When a crisis hit, I fell to my knees and gave that burden over to God, only to take back the reins of my life as soon as things calmed down. I wanted those times when I surrendered and submitted to God to be the norm, not the exception. But I also knew myself well enough to understand that without a plan, I would never get there. At least not for long.

How *would* I get there? Was it even possible?

My mind began considering possibilities as I prayed and labored on my exercise machine.

Being a visual person and a lover of sappy movies, I immediately recalled a scene from the Jim Carrey comedy *Bruce Almighty*. Next thing I knew, I was tapping my cell phone screen, switching from my Bible app to YouTube. It didn't take long for me to find the scene that came to mind. The surrender scene.

In the movie, Jim Carrey's character, Bruce, is given the power of God Almighty. He starts out by carrying on some tomfoolery, answers the desperate prayers of those who want to lose weight on the Krispy Kreme diet, and tries to win the affections of a beautiful woman. But what he ultimately ends up doing is making himself miserable and destroying the relationship with that special woman. When Bruce finally realizes that he is failing at trying to be God, he gives the whole mess over to Him.

I watched the surrender scene and sobbed over the image of a rain-drenched Bruce Almighty kneeling in the middle of the highway, arms stretched to heaven, pleading with God to take over. He didn't want to be God anymore. "You win!" he shouts to the sky. "I surrender to your will."

That was what I wanted. That was what I'd been asking God for. What I needed. In order to know God better and stop the frustrating cycle of control, I needed to surrender completely.

As I turned off the video and wiped my eyes, I realized that I desperately needed to learn to let go of the reins. I wanted to learn to let God control my future. I wanted to relinquish and stop fighting back and forth. I wanted to get to a place where I naturally submitted to His will each day—to identify what was getting in my way and then surrender those areas of control to my God.

But my life wasn't like a movie where all of my issues would be resolved after one dramatic scene. Surrendering would require a great deal of discipline. It would require prayer, fasting, and a commitment to making changes as I allowed God to search my heart.

I thought about Jesus's forty days in the wilderness and realized, *That's it!*

That prayer on my cross trainer inspired me to devote forty days to complete surrender. The results were life changing. Now I invite you to experience the same freedom through your own journey of surrender.

Are you ready?

To know Him more?

To give Him complete control?

To make Him your Lord?

See what amazing things happen when you trust Him with everything.

How to Use This Study

40 Days of Surrender is a deep dive, using the steps that I took while learning to submit and give everything to God. It will help you to identify areas where you need to relinquish control or where you repeatedly struggle. The goal of this study is to point you toward the Source of freedom and equip you with tools of spiritual discipline and deep connection with the One who knows exactly how to guide you and change your heart.

My prayer is that the process will provide you with a new and fresh direction as you let go of control and let God lead every area of your life.

Here are the steps that you will take in each four-day section:

Day 1: Pray and Meditate
The most effective prayers are done in earnest. On Day 1 of each section, challenge yourself to take at least ten minutes to pray for that week's focus. You will find a short written prayer to get you started. Once you feel that God has shown you something to work on, chronicle it in the space provided. If you need more than those few lines, feel free to write more in your journal.

Day 2: Fast/Sacrifice
The next step is to fast. I am recommending a twenty-four-hour fast from food one day a week during your forty days of surrender. You can fast from dinner to dinner, or breakfast, lunch, and dinner on one day. Be sure to drink plenty of water during this time.

Prior to fasting, it would be wise for you to check with your healthcare provider or physician, especially if you've never fasted before. Please also consider any health issues that you know will be impacted by lack of food (for example, if you are diabetic, pregnant, or have been advised not to skip meals). If you cannot fast from food due to a health issue, or if your doctor advises against it, please do what is best for your body. In this case, I challenge you to fast from a favorite treat or comfort food. So if you love coffee, diet soda, or cookies, eliminate it for the twenty-four-hour fasting period. Another option would be to fast from social media, television, your smartphone, or something else that you run to for escape, comfort, or distraction. Some people even fast from talking for a day so they can listen to God. The point is to sacrifice a fleshly desire and let God fill the empty place. You will discover that honoring Him in this way and drawing closer to Him in moments of hunger or weakness leads to profound growth.

Day 3: Identify

While fasting and praying through each topic, you will find yourself identifying things that you need to change, let go of, or relinquish control over and give to the Lord. Invite God to bring to mind what needs to change in order for Him to do His best work in you. Be sure to record this process throughout the week. If you run out of room in the space provided and record what He reveals to you in your journal. These days might be good times to share what you're uncovering with a trusted friend or small group and let them pray for you.

Day 4: Take Action

It's one thing to recognize a problem and another to take steps toward solving it. Once you've identified an area that needs to change, it's time for action. For each thing God asks you to surrender or relinquish control of, write down what you'll do to make it a reality. Maybe you'll plan to ask a friend to hold you accountable, schedule a more consistent quiet time, or seek counseling. Write the plan down as a reminder and also as a record of your growth.

To make this study easy to follow, I broke it down into sections that cover four days each. We will examine a variety of topics including the heart of your faith, insecurities, children and family, friendship, ministry, finances, physical health, and recognizing your "signature sin."

How about taking a few moments to lay the next forty days before God? Ask Him to make you open and receptive to what He wants to reveal to you. Thank Him in advance for what you will gain on the path to surrender.

The Heart of Your Faith
Days 1-4

Search me, God, and know my heart; test me and know my anxious thoughts. See if there is any offensive way in me, and lead me in the way everlasting.
Psalm 139:23–24

Many of us, especially those of us who've attended church for a long time, have heard the challenging question: "If you were on trial for being a Christian, would there be enough evidence to convict you?"

The first time I heard the statement above, I got nervous and did a mental inventory of my life. I thought about my Bible, which was on the shelf. I read it regularly, at least most of the time. That had to count for something. Then I considered my Sunday church attendance. That definitely counted as Christian activity. But what about my small wooden *Bless This Home* plaque in the living room? Would that give me away as a believer or just someone who enjoyed inspirational décor? I considered running out and buying one of those silver fish-shaped bumper stickers and slapping it on the back of my car. Everyone I passed while driving would know without a doubt, *She's a Jesus follower*. But then I thought about my late-for-an-appointment driving habits and dismissed the idea.

Next, I considered the verbal evidence that could be held against me and came to the immediate conclusion that I definitely sounded like a Christian. I could hold my own in a theological discussion, and many women came to me for advice and prayer.

I handled crises like a good Christian girl. At least, most of the time. I never prayed more than when life was falling apart at the seams.

While contemplating my faith during my first few days of surrender, however, I sensed God telling me to go deeper. It was time to make a nonverbal statement in the journey of my faith that went beyond the content of my walls and shelves. One that meant something. I didn't want to just look like a believer or sound like a strong woman of faith; I wanted to live like one.

Sure, I had a Bible. I had several. But did my life reflect its teachings?

Going to church was great, but did I apply the sermons to my behavior and attitude once I left the parking lot?

Which said more about my commitment to live like Jesus: a bumper sticker or my driving habits? Or what about how I responded to other drivers—the ones who cut me off or failed to go through the intersection as soon as the light turned green? That probably said even more.

If someone put me on trial for being a Christian, I wanted them to have more than an attendance record and knickknacks to hold against me. I was sick and tired of good enough faith, the faith that got me down the road, allowed me to sound wise and deep in discussions about Scripture, and drove people to come to me when they had a need. I wanted my faith to be genuine. My experience on the cross trainer, weeping over a Jim Carrey movie, had left me hovering at the point of surrender, knowing change would require a daily dying of my flesh on all levels and in all areas of my life.

If you are reading this book, you are probably in a similar place of longing to go deeper with God. Maybe you've tried changing certain areas of your life—your response when things don't go your way, a bad habit or persistent fear, expectations of your kids or husband that have more to do with your desires than God's—only to take them up again. Or maybe there are areas of your faith that look super spiritual on the outside, while your heart tells a different story.

As I learned, genuine faith requires genuine surrender. It often calls us to closely examine our faith and identify what is holding us back. It means allowing God into the heart of our faith (which He knows anyway) and seeing how it impacts our thoughts, behaviors, and goals. For me it was areas of pride and control. For you it might be something different.

Keep in mind that surrender is a process. Like any kind of change, it takes time. We have setback and restarts, but that's where grace comes in.

If surrender has been an ongoing struggle for you, ask God to use the next forty days to help you let go once and for all. If surrender is a new concept, ask Him to help you see the benefits in giving everything to the Lord.

I created this as an all-in study and encourage you to approach it that way as well. If God brings something to mind, no matter how small, or no matter how desperately you want to exclude it, let Him work. Commit to hold nothing back. Trust me, it will be worth it. During these forty days, we are asking God to examine our hearts, to reveal our flaws, and to test us.

The first four days will focus on giving Him full rein over the process. Settle into your favorite quiet time spot and ask Him to fill you with expectancy and excitement for the work you will do together.

Day 1: Pray for ten minutes without interruption

God, I open my life to You. I ask You to examine my heart. Show me the errors of my ways—the areas where my faith has been little more than a good show. Inspect the innermost corners of my heart, Lord. Reveal the ugly pride and inconsistencies. Open the sealed box of hurt, sin, and rebellion. I give You my life, Lord. Change me, mold me, help me. I am Yours, Lord. Amen.

Write down a few things that God reveals to you as you pray.
- ○ _____
- ○ _____
- ○ _____

Day 2: Fast/Sacrifice

Do this for twenty-four hours (no food, but liquids are okay, and definitely drink water). Remember, if your health prevents you from fasting from food, you may sacrifice something else.

Write down what God reveals to you during the fast.
- ○ _____
- ○ _____
- ○ _____

Day 3: Identify

Write down an area of inconsistency that God has brought to mind or aspects of your faith that aren't as genuine as you'd like them to be.
- ○ _____
- ○ _____
- ○ _____

Day 4: Take action

What do you plan to do now that you know what needs to change?
- ○ _____
- ○ _____
- ○ _____

The Heart of Your Faith: Other Women's Stories

Sheila

I have failed myself miserably trying to be what others wanted me to be. My desire to have everyone like me (which is impossible) turned me into a people pleaser.

At age seventeen I met Jesus in a little Pentecostal church. He washed my sins away that day and gave me a clean slate. I remember feeling so overwhelmed with joy that I seemed to be flying high. I could not tell enough people about my experience. My grannies, who had set a faithful Christian example for me all of my life, were thrilled. But my friends at high school called me a Jesus freak when I talked about Him or mentioned the Bible. They ridiculed me when I went to church during the week instead of a school activity. As time went on, I started straddling the fence, with one foot on the Lord's side and the other in the world with my friends. I began going to parties and drinking. This fence straddling carried on for most of my life. I was torn between fully living for Jesus and pleasing my friends and acquaintances.

I was a fake. But He never gave up on me. I have witnessed and experienced God's relentless pursuit of me again and again. When I am on a path that He does not want for me, He gently, or sometimes abruptly, throws a roadblock in my way that redirects me to listen. Yes, there has been heartache and times of deep pain, shame, guilt, and regret. Through the years, though, the Lord has helped me be true to myself and stop worrying about what others think. I have learned to focus on pleasing my Savior, the One who gave His life for me.

Rose

Few things test faith more than having a dying child. Each time I looked into my frail son's drawn face I saw the pallor of death. In 2000, his doctor told him he was next on the list to have a liver transplant. Then something went wrong, and he was not chosen next. After three days of waiting with bags packed, he found out his lab work did not meet their stringent requirements. When I heard this devastating news, I felt my world spin out of control. How could this happen? I laid on my bed and cried out in agony. With choking sobs, I prayed to the Lord: You have saved his life five times. You must have a reason, so why not this time? Please save him again.

My son was given a liver transplant within twenty-four hours. I was elated. God had answered my cries.

Twenty years later, his liver is still functioning normally. The doctors call him a miracle because most people don't live this long after a liver transplant.

This experience is my reminder to put my faith in the Lord and have confidence that the God of today still performs miracles.

Amelia

While many women pride themselves on being able to multitask, I find that by doing two things at once I don't give either my full attention, so I miss important details. Recently, I thought about my tendency to do this with God. How can I say He is the heart of my faith if He isn't worthy of my focus? Why do I let little things distract me from Him or be more important than listening to Him? I know God is always there to hear me, but shouldn't I always be there to listen to Him?

While working in my yard, I noticed that my beautiful tulip tree was in full bloom. The gentle breeze was causing my blooms to flutter. It was pretty to see, but then as I watched, I realized that the gentle breeze was loosening the flower petals. As I mowed the lawn, I saw that it was covered with petals. Those petals reminded me of the time I spend with God. It's beautiful when I'm in full bloom and

I am focused on Him, but as those little breezes come and distract me, my focus fades. I shift my focus and I become weaker, and my petals start to fall.

This moment reminded me of my need to keep my times with Him protected from the breezes that can so easily pull me away. It's time to stop multitasking my faith.

Kathi

I've been clean and sober a long time, but while getting clean, I leaned on myself and others for support. I didn't bring God along the rocky road with me until I achieved sobriety. Even then, trusting God took me a while. Now that God is finally with me, I see Him healing me from my tumultuous past.

I've learned that getting clean doesn't mean my life suddenly becomes perfect. I had struggles that left me almost catatonic and unable to move. But when I finally mustered up the courage and, little by little, trusted God, I got out of my toxic home and rebuilt my life. He put wonderful people in my life who loved me for who I was. He sent friends who didn't judge me for my past. I never had that kind of unconditional love from the people I grew up with. I now cling to the Scripture below:

"Trust in the LORD with all your heart; do not depend on your own understanding. Seek his will in all you do, and he will show you which path to take" (Proverbs 3:5–6 NLT).

I have no idea what God has in mind for me next, but I know I can trust Him.

Mary

I have a terrible habit of doing just enough to get by. At the same time, I condemn others for starting a job and not finishing it. Of course I've been guilty of the same thing, so my solution is to avoid starting in the first place, convincing myself that if I don't start, I don't have to worry about not finishing. But then nothing gets done at all. I never make any progress. Ultimately, I wind up feeling discouraged and like a failure.

I know I can change the story I tell myself at any time. I must remember that progress is just that: progress. By taking one step at a time, I will make a difference over time. I refuse to let Satan guide my journey by buying into his lies. The Lord is with me on each endeavor, and He is the One I am following now.

Sophie
Letter to Self

My precious child,

I have loved you from the very moment of your creation. You entered the world innocently, curiously, fully open to My glorious plan for you.

As you grew, I led you to discover all of My creations—the warmth of the morning sun on your face, the smell of flowers and salty sea air, the feel of soft puppy fur under your tiny hands, and the comfort of a gentle hug. I surrounded you with a family to love, guide, and protect you. Your little-girl prayers and innocence melted My heart.

Your independent nature nudged you away from Me, and your desire to seek Me in prayer gave way to the influence of friends and schoolmates, teachers, and television. Still, I delighted in watching you read stories about tiny people under the floorboards and time travel through a tesseract, sliding into the big pool at Pine Grove, and riding your bike to school for the first time with your best friend and stopping to buy candy on the way home.

You felt My calming presence at your first Holy Communion and when you sang hymns in church, singing your favorites extra loud.

I instilled a kind and gentle heart in you and a fondness for things you could love and help: lost puppies, overturned bugs, and unpopular friends.

You pushed hard to succeed, trading rest and time in prayer with Me for the desire to fit in, be the smartest, and get the best parts. You ignored My gentle guidance to slow down and care for your heart and body and refused to accept your physical limitations.

Exhausted and undernourished, your body failed and your dream crashed down. Spirit and body broken, emotions walled in, you gave your heart away to a boy when you were far too young and then to a man who wasn't ready to love and care for you the way I could. I lamented first the loss of your childlike innocence and then the sorrow of your grownup heartbreak. I answered your prayers with a way out and covered you in love and acceptance. You suffered greatly, but you trusted in Me.

We shared many carefree days as our relationship was renewed. As you studied My Word and learned to praise Me, I faithfully sprinkled new blessings throughout your life: talents, friendships, experiences.

When a new love came into your life, you were swept away by materialism. You struggled with perfectionism, and worry haunted you, but I blessed you with a beautiful home and a precious son and daughter. Through your children I reminded you of the innocence and beauty of unconditional love. You taught them to love deeply, to reach out for the less fortunate, to care for My creations, and to appreciate sunsets and smiles. I wished you had shared My Word with them more often, but there is still time.

Again and again I have shown you that I am faithful, that I will never forsake you, and still you are reluctant to relinquish control. With each affliction, I patiently wait and gently guide your footsteps back to My path for you.

My child, My own, surrender your worries and struggles, and trust the path of peace that I have laid out before you. It is time.

Welcome home.

My Inner Thirteen-Year-Old
Days 5–8

The LORD appeared to us in the past, saying: "I have loved you with an everlasting love; I have drawn you with unfailing kindness."
Jeremiah 31:3

In junior high, I attended every class with the same group of kids. All of their families were members of the same synagogue and socialized at the same country club. Every Monday morning, I overheard talk about weekend parties that I never got invited to. My family was Italian, Catholic, and did not belong to the country club, all of which disqualified me from the cool group. I was an outcast, practically an alien. A non-person. Instead of passing notes about where to meet after school and who was going out with whom, I paid attention in class, did well in school, and silently went through my lonely days.

My lack of a social life paid off when I was selected to attend an honors science camp. Two students from each class were chosen, and for the first time, that chosen few included me. The five-star camp was top rated and immersed students in botany, astronomy, microscopy, and ecology.

This was the opportunity of a lifetime—a dream of mine. The school district was even paying my way. I wouldn't have been able to go otherwise. Although my parents did all right financially, we lived on a tight budget with my father working and my mother a stay-at-home mom. I was one of four children, so one income had to go a long way.

During science camp, I gained the attention of a certain boy from school. He was cute, smart, funny, and a member of the clique that my classmates had shut me out of. During a night hike to view the constellations, he held my hand as we walked the moonlit path to the top of the mountain. I felt like an angel. Friendless me had been chosen once again, this time by one of the most popular guys in my class! But whenever the other kids from school saw me talking to him, they jeered and gave me hateful looks.

Things went from bad to worse when we returned to school. The clique openly humiliated and bullied me daily. They warned me, "You better stay away from him, or you'll regret it. You think we've made life hard for you now? Well, just you wait. Stay away from him!"

I didn't understand what I had done that was so wrong. He'd pursued *me*. He told me I was cute. He said he liked me. Were the other girls jealous? Was that why they were being so mean?

One day this boy cornered me in the courtyard, his entourage behind him. He looked down at the dirt and sheepishly said, "I just want you to know that I never really liked you. The whole thing at camp was a joke." He looked back at his friends, then at me. "I think you're a dog."

His friends laughed.

Shocked and crying, my cheeks blazing red, I ran off, leaving their victorious laughter in the distance. To say I was devastated would be an understatement. I felt certain that his horribly cruel comment must be true. To everyone but my family, I was unlovable, an outcast, and sinfully ugly. A dog.

Thankfully, my parents moved to Orange County that summer. I started my freshman year with no friends. No past, no present, no identity, and no clique taunting me between classes. It was a chance to start all over.

I attended the first dance with a few nice girls from my class. At first I stood on the sidelines, listening to a live band play Top 40 songs. Someone tapped my shoulder. When I turned around, I saw a guy standing there.

"Would you like to dance?" he asked.

I froze and looked around him, expecting to see a group of laughing friends. I wasn't going to fall victim to his plan. Not this time. I was the dog who no boy would ever want.

"Who put you up to this?" I asked.

He looked bewildered and shook his head. "What do you mean?"

"So this isn't a joke."

He shook his head. "No. I really do want to dance with you."

I shrugged, feeling a little embarrassed. "Oh. Okay."

We ended up dancing and having a good time, but though it felt nice to know he must have thought I was somewhat cute, I never did get over the feeling of being less than okay when it came to guys. It took me many years, a lot of really stupid choices, and escaping an abusive marriage for me to finally realize that I was acceptable.

I believe that a wounded thirteen-year-old hides within many women. A junior high girl who doesn't think she is good enough, is desperate to feel loved and valued, and will seek it at any cost. It's this lack of self-esteem that often causes women to become promiscuous, fall for and stay with abusive men, or commit to relationships that are not equally yoked. It caused me to get trapped in an abusive marriage. But as I've learned, when we experience the love of Jesus and discover what it truly means to be cherished, we can start to find freedom in our relationships.

Now that I am an adult and have taken time to heal, my friendships and views of romance are no longer driven by teenage insecurities. After surviving a horrible first marriage that almost cost me my life, I have a wonderful partnership that has survived, even thrived, over thirty-two years so far.

But even in a marriage founded on Christ and our mutual love for each other, I faced new challenges. During my forty days of surrender, God revealed to me that now that I'm no longer living with a bully, I've gotten in a habit of wanting to be in control. I catch myself struggling to allow my husband to lead as the head of our household while

I support him as God intended. Not as a doormat, but as a helpmate. Letting God change me in this area continues to be the cry of my heart.

What is your biggest challenge this week when it comes to feeling loved or acceptable? What memories, wounds, or lies might God be asking you to surrender so you can move forward? What are you trying to control to avoid getting hurt? As you go into this week, ask God to hold you especially close as you let Him examine and tend to these deep areas of your heart.

Day 5: Pray for ten minutes without interruption.

God, You know all the ways that I've been hurt, the reasons behind my poor choices, and even the story behind my need for control. I give those pieces of my life to You today.
Lead me into the relationships that are found in You and help me to trust them. Help me to push away relationships that are unhealthy or abusive or which distract me from my walk with You. I give you permission to reveal the areas where I'm guilty of controlling others out of fear or because I'm giving in to old insecurities. Help me to be the woman You designed me to be. Lead me, oh Lord. Amen.

Write down a few things that God reveals to you as you pray.
- _____
- _____
- _____

Day 6: Fast/Sacrifice for twenty-four hours.

Write down what God reveals to you during the fast.
- _____
- _____
- _____

Day 7: Identify

Write down the area of control, insecurity, or unhealthy relational patterns that God is asking you to surrender.

- _____
- _____
- _____

Day 8: Take action

What do you plan to do now that you know what needs to change?

- _____
- _____
- _____

My Inner Thirteen-Year-Old: Other Women's Stories

Rose

When my twin brother and I were eight years old, my parents went to town and left us alone. While they were gone, two male family friends came over, and one of them sexually abused me. My brother and I swore to never tell anyone. I kept it a secret until I was in my fifties. This event changed my life and how I viewed relationships with both men and women. It affected my confidence and self- image.

I learned later that children who experience this kind of abuse either become celibate or promiscuous. I went down the road of looking for love in the wrong places and became sexually active at a very young age. This led to a pattern of repeat betrayals and inability to trust anyone, including God.

Healing began when I got a job with the health department and saw a film about rape. All the emotions came flooding back and I started crying. After a lot of counseling, I am completely healed and at peace. Finally, I understand how my secret and the bondage of shame and fear kept me from having a relationship with my heavenly Father. I thank Him for answering my prayers for healing.

Amelia

I grew up in the 1950s, 1960s, and 1970s, when divorce wasn't as common as it is now. In those days, it carried a stigma. My parents divorced when I was just three years old and my brother was five. Mom worked hard to support us, often working two jobs. At a time when most kids came home from school to a snack, my brother and I came home to an empty house. My father, who was in the military and moved often, chose not to be a part of our lives. I heard other kids talk about their dads. It seemed like all the school functions were attended by both parents, so I spent a lot of time feeling like an outcast.

I was the kid who just didn't fit in. I was singled out and bullied over and over again. In seventh grade, at the time when my body was going through all of those hormonal changes, the bullying was worse than ever.

When I started struggling with spelling, one of my male teachers offered to help me after school. But instead of just tutoring me, he became sexually inappropriate with me. Though it made me feel uncomfortable, I trusted him when he said, "Don't worry." He was a teacher. Someone other than my mom wanted me. My seventh-grade brain told me that it was okay to keep this secret. I had no idea that what was going on would be considered abuse. It went on for two years.

My mom knew that someone had a hold on me but couldn't get the truth out of me, so she reached out to my father and I went to live with him. Though this allowed me to have a fresh start, I also learned that my father did not have the skills to be the dad I'd been longing for. He had a truck stop and put me to work there. He and his wife often left the responsibility of running it over to me for days so they could go out of town. Once again, adult men started to "befriend" me in the same way that the teacher did.

The cycle repeated itself in my twenties. It took me a long time to figure out that I was looking for a fatherly love that I had heard about but never had.

God helped me realize that I was seeking someone to make me feel complete and "normal."

During this time of surrender, God opened my eyes and reminded me that He created me with a purpose. In Him I am perfect, not "normal." I can only find peace and happiness if I seek Him and follow the path He wants for my life. I now feel ready to do that.

Jeanine

It was the night of my bachelorette party, and I realized I was probably making a mistake. Everyone thought it was so cute that my fiancé and I opted for a combined bachelor/bachelorette party by having dinner together before going our separate ways to have fun with our friends. The truth was, I was afraid to let him be away from me for too long and either go into a rage and end up getting arrested or cheat on me.

I had met him as a teenager and immediately fell in love with his assertive yet vulnerable side. He was the light of my life, and I thought the sun rose and set with him. He was smart, funny, sarcastic, and deep. He was wounded in ways that spoke to me. I thought I could heal him. Even through years of his drug addiction, disloyalty, anger, and abuse, he was my everything. I always found ways to blame myself for what had happened and looked for ways to be "enough" for him: putting him through school so he could get a degree and finally feel better about himself, moving to another state to start over, giving him a beautiful baby to raise. None of it worked.

My marriage started to end the night that our daughter was born by emergency C-section. My mom had been the one to comfort me while my husband made a playlist. In the OR, when my blood pressure tanked, a nurse offered sweet words as I tried not to pass out, but my husband said nothing. When my beautiful daughter was placed in my arms, I cried, realizing I finally understood what true love meant and felt completely whole. I looked at my husband, expecting to see the same look on his face, only to be met with blankness.

I had a series of complications at the hospital and at home, which only made my husband mad. That was when the truth finally set in. I stayed with him for eleven months after our daughter was born, then I moved back home to California, defeated. I'd done everything I could to make him happy, but I'd failed. It was then that I looked down at my precious daughter. I weighed, with a heavy heart, divorce versus her seeing and learning that women should be treated badly.

It took those years of abuse for me to finally realize that maybe I was enough. If I wanted to be a role model for my daughter, I needed to love myself.

God continues to use my daughter to show me that I am good, that I am strong, and that I can survive anything life throws at me.

Lord, My Child Belongs to You

DAYS 9–12

*"I prayed for this child, and the L*ORD *has granted me what I asked of him. So now I give him to the L*ORD*. For his whole life he will be given over to the L*ORD*." And he worshiped the L*ORD *there.*

1 Samuel 1:27–28

While growing up, I had a large extended family and a happy home life. My childhood included very little drama other than the typical sibling rivalry and "But all my friends get to go" battles. I only remember one or two arguments between my parents, so I know they got along well most days. I had very few complaints. We enjoyed the excitement of Christmas mornings and went on family summer vacations. All of this felt normal to me. I couldn't wait to have children of my own and recreate the same happy life for them that I'd had.

Then I left home and discovered that other women had very different experiences. When I was in college, for example, I worked as a waitress and met two young hostesses who were roommates. While getting to know them, I learned that both women had fled their family homes in search of a better life. One had left a physically abusive mother, the other a sexually abusive father. I cringed over their stories, thankful for the peaceful childhood I'd had. When I had kids, I would never let anyone hurt them.

Escaping an abusive marriage only made me more determined to give any future children I had the best life possible. I now knew through experience that life could be dangerous and scary, and I was determined to make sure that my children did not experience the horrific tumult that I had endured. In my new life with Sam, though I could celebrate a healthy marriage and a Spirit-filled faith walk, I was still plagued with baggage and dragged issues from my past. One huge hurdle was struggling for years with infertility. When I finally became pregnant, we were thrilled over the arrival of our twins—a boy and a girl. We named them Samuel and Jessica.

After all that waiting, I felt like Hannah—so much so that I surrendered Samuel and Jessica to God as my offerings. I boldly declared to my Christian friends that my children belonged to the Lord, that they were in His hands.

I must confess, however, that my trust lasted until one or both of my twins got sick, I heard a frightening statistic on television, someone hurt their feelings, or a new skill (such as riding a two-wheeler) led to injury. In those sleepless nights of treating fevers and coughs, and the moments of drying "She was so mean" tears and bandaging boo-boos that could've been worse, Samuel and Jessica became *my* kids. After all, no one knew or could love them better than their mother, right? It became my job to shelter and protect them, to keep them well, out of harm's way, and wound free.

On carefree days when they had the same fun I'd had as a child, managed to dodge the latest stomach bug, and mastered a kid-skill without falling down, they were God's again. "I trust Him fully," I boasted to the other moms.

In other words, deep in my heart, I only trusted God with Samuel and Jessica as long as He was blessing and protecting them.

It wasn't until Samuel suffered a concussion so severe that it altered his behavior for weeks that I found myself face down before God. I cried out to Him to heal Samuel and return him to his old, normal self. He was the only One who could make my son well again. With all that I had, sobbing from the depths of my heart, I gave my son to God. For real this time. The longer I prayed, the more I realized that there was no way I could ever love my son more than the One who'd created him. God loved me and my son so much that He gave us His Son. He loved my children more than I could imagine. I knew that no matter what, Samuel would be okay.

That day, I intentionally submitted and surrendered Samuel's future—each second, minute, day, week, year, and decade—to my Lord. Good or bad, hurt or well. Samuel was his.

No matter what kind of childhood we had, once we become parents, we want a good life for our children. We want to place them in the Lord's hands, say "They're yours," and know for sure they'll be safe. Instead, we learn that saying "My child is in God's hands" is easy until our words are put to the test.

Often, it takes a crisis for us to understand that there actually is someone who knows and loves our children more than we do: their Creator. When we entrust our kids to Him, we place them in the hands of the Father who knows them best and has a purpose for every moment of their life.

What test of surrender are you facing right now when it comes to your kids? Maybe your child is sick or is about to start school with a special need. Perhaps you just found out that your daughter experienced a trauma that you couldn't protect her from. If you don't have children, maybe God is asking you to surrender your longing for one. He might also place another loved one on your heart. As you approach the next four days and loosen your grip on those you love, ask Him to help you grasp His deep love for them.

Day 9: Pray for ten minutes without interruption

God, I open my life to You as I learn to trust You with those I love. Help me to understand that You love my family more than I could ever fathom. Reveal the areas where I try to control their future. Help me to understand that You created them. You allowed me to be their mother (or insert sibling, daughter, aunt, wife, or whatever applies to your situation). Help me to give up the unhealthy struggles of control. Help me to trust You, dear Lord. Thank You for being a trustworthy Father.

Write down a few things that God reveals to you as you pray.
- ○ _____
- ○ _____
- ○ _____

Day 10: Fast/Sacrifice for twenty-four hours

Write down what God reveals to you during the fast.
- ○ _____
- ○ _____
- ○ _____

Day 11: Identify

Write down your fears and concerns regarding your children (or loved one).
- ○ _____
- ○ _____
- ○ _____

Day 12: Take action

What do you plan to do differently now that you know what needs to change?
- ○ _____
- ○ _____
- ○ _____

"Lord, My Child Belongs to You": Other Women's Stories

Amelia

I thought I was content with my life as a single woman. I knew my life was supposed to be this way. Yet when I tell others that I'm single, I feel like I haven't lived as rich and full a life as those who are married and have kids. So I guess that is what God is asking me to surrender: the children and family I never had.

Once again, I must remind myself that God has a plan for my life as a single woman. I have heard the sermons and lessons that we can't all be the hands because then there wouldn't be any arms, or eyes, or lungs, so why do I let myself feel less valuable because I have a different lifestyle than other women? It's the life He created me to live.

As I go through the aging process and look back on my life, I see that God was always there for me. I made it through some very difficult times and know He has used me. So why, when I get to know new people and they ask me about my marriage and kids, and I tell them that I'm single, do I find myself feeling as if I am not as valuable as they are—that my life is less because I don't have what they have?

I need to be proud of who God made me to be. When someone asks me about my kids or husband, how I reply should reflect that. God is showing me that as I surrender this area of insecurity to Him, I need to choose my words wisely when talking to others. It's time for my response to send a message not only to them, but also to myself.

When someone asks about children and I say, "Oh, I never married or had children," I feel as if I failed. Why do I feel that way? I knew that I wouldn't be a wife or mother. That isn't who God made me to be. How could I have failed by being wise enough to follow the wisdom God gave me?

Now when people ask me about my children or a mate, I need to answer differently. I need to show them what God has given me instead of what I don't have. What if I were to say, "I don't have any of my own children, but God made me an aunt and a great-aunt, and sometimes other people's kids call me Grandma"?

Wow, just saying that makes me feel blessed, not less valuable. My prayer is that I will remember all He has given me. God doesn't ask me to follow society's plan. He asks me to follow His plan. And so far, His plan for me has been wonderful.

Mary

At age seventeen, on my first date with the man who would later become my husband, I said I didn't want to have children. I didn't expect to ever want them. Then we got married, and after being married a year, I realized I did want to have children. Our feelings can be so fickle.

My husband and I tried for a long time to get pregnant. We went through testing and even used fertility drugs and temperature charts. After a few years of trying, I took a month off work and volunteered to help in the kitchen during our church's summer camp. I needed a break from the stress of focusing on having a baby. In a way, this was my form of surrender. The work was exhausting, but I had a wonderful time in a fun environment. A couple of months later, we were pregnant—without drugs or temp charts. What a blessing.

Four years and six days later, we received another blessing. Then four years and six months after that, we had our surprise child. We're so thankful. We went from barren to bountiful. My cup overflowed. I will never forget the tears and anguish of struggling to get pregnant. My whole world was centered on having a precious child. When I took that break from trying and put my whole heart into serving, God brought me out of the desert to the oasis that included a better plan than I originally hoped for. I remember this whenever He asks me to surrender something or someone I love.

Days 13-16

The righteous choose their friends carefully, but the way of the wicked leads them astray.

Proverbs 12:26

Friends. We make them in preschool, chase them in kindergarten, play with them in grade school, form groups with them in junior high and high school, and hopefully find lifelong healthy friends in college. Sometimes we are fortunate enough to have a friendship that lasts from childhood through adulthood. Forming good, long-lasting, close friendships is rare and valuable. It's something I've learned to cherish.

Throughout our lives we also learn the importance of obeying Scripture's instruction to choose our friends wisely. We experience the truth behind the warning that bad company corrupts morals. Those of us who grew up in the church received regular reminders that we must be in the world but not of it. But experience is the best teacher when it comes to learning what that means and how to wisely select an intimate inner circle of close friends.

I had a lesson in this several years ago. I'm not sure why, but my family always seemed to move on rainy days. As we pulled into the small town of 800 people after leaving a large city of over 300,000, I felt as dreary as the weather. We'd left our church, our small group, and a tight group of friends behind. It didn't take long for our family to get invited to social events, pool parties, and barbecues, for cocktails, and to join friends for dinners at the local eatery. Our new friends didn't attend church, but we continued to, so we didn't give our time with them a second thought. It was wonderful to be in a group that had fun together. They'd welcomed us, Sammy, Jessi, Sarah and Mandi Sammy, Jessi, Sarah and Mandi had kids to play with, and we felt like part of the community.

But I was shocked by how quickly my moral compass began to slide. The women were nice, but when we got together, our conversations degraded quickly to gossip about the other couples. Flirtatious behaviors, inappropriate jokes, and spicy language were the norm. Before I knew it, I was behaving just like them.

It repulsed me to recognize that I could change in a few months. One day I realized that I could not be part of this group anymore. So I stopped accepting invitations. After a while, the invitations stopped coming. I became an island of a woman, alone with no friends except for my husband. But God had His hand on me. Although I didn't find a close friend for years, I got many opportunities to serve at our new church, my husband and I got connected to a small group, and we started to form relationships that were grounded in Jesus.

Flash forward to my kids' freshman year in high school. I was at a track meet, shifting my weight on the hard bleachers, wishing I'd brought a bleacher chair and an umbrella to block the hot Central California sun. God had answered my prayers and provided a faith-based high school for my twins to attend. We commuted twenty-five miles so they could be here. For Samuel and Jessica, track was a new sport. I watched them on the track field with several other teens milling about. They didn't seem to have problems making new friends and mixing in. But as a freshman mom, I didn't know anyone.

Wistfully, I watched the other moms engage in casual chatter. Some were toting little ones, and others were managing backpacks, but all were doing so among friends. I watched one woman bound up the bleachers and approach a group, move to another group, and then to another. Then, in a bold move I've still not mastered, this dark-haired beauty with an inviting smile trudged up the last few steps and stopped right in front of me.

"You must be a new mom. I've never seen you before." She reached out to shake my hand. "I'm Cathy. Which one of the runners is yours?"

I pointed out my twins, then she told me which kids were hers. As we got to know each other, we discovered that both of us were married and had four children. We both wanted to encourage our sons and daughters to make Christ the center of their lives. That one encounter grew into a weaving of two families.

Cathy has been my pillar, my cheerleader, and my inspiration. She challenges me to try new things, to assess my faith, and to grow in my marriage and parenting.

I continue to be drawn to Cathy's solid priorities: God, her husband, her children, friends, and work. In that order. For so long I hoped for a friendship that would withstand the test of time. A friend who I could be transparent with, who would know all of me and still like me. God answered that prayer through Cathy. We've prayed together, joyfully praised the blessings in each other's lives, and have held one another up through times when we could not breathe.

We've shared the victories and challenges of every day, from praying for our wayward offspring, to blowing out more candles each year, to burying our parents. Through all this, she loves me, and loves her God more, and I feel the same about her. For that I will be eternally grateful.

I often wonder what might have happened if I'd clung to that original group of friends instead of letting go. I might have become even more like them. One thing I do know: I would have missed out on my friendship with Cathy.

What comes to mind when you think about friendship? Are you still waiting for that rare bond with a sister in Christ? Or is God asking you to let go of a friendship that isn't good for you? Whatever your friendship story looks like right now, take a moment to ask God to help you lay it in His hands.

Day 13: Pray for ten minutes without interruption

God, I submit to You now. You know my history with friendships, my desires, and my hurts. Give me the strength to let go of unhealthy friendships and nurture the healthy ones, even if it means having fewer people in my social circle. Lord, I ask You to also help me be a good friend. Show me how to love others as You love them and to see in each of them the heart that You see. I seek You, Lord, to be the center of my friendships. Thank you, Lord.

Write down a few things that God reveals to you about friendships.
- _____
- _____
- _____

Day 14: Fast/Sacrifice for twenty-four hours

Write down what God reveals to you during the fast.
- _____
- _____
- _____

Day 15: Identify

Write down some friendship patterns or desires that God is asking you to change or give over to Him.
- _____
- _____
- _____

Day 16: Take action
What do you plan to do differently now that God has made things clearer?
- _____
- _____
- _____

My BFF: Other Women's Stories

Rachel

I faintly remember the first friend I had when I was four years old. Her name was Lisa, and she lived across the street from us in San Jose, where I was born. I remember playing in the front yard with her. When I was five, my family moved to Lodi, so I never saw Lisa again, but I still have happy memories of playing with her as a little girl.

I had friends growing up, but I was in and out of the hospital, which made it hard to have a best friend. The stories I needed to share were not conversation topics that the average preteen girl enjoyed. I found I could connect deeply with the girls I was in treatment with, who were usually older than me. But then we got discharged and lost touch.

As an adult, it is even more difficult for me to find friends. I reach out to other women, but they don't reciprocate. If I do find a friend, it never grows beyond the surface. It used to bother me. I would beat myself up and wonder if there was something wrong with me. But I did a lot of soul searching and eventually realized that as long as I reach out, I am doing all I can to foster a relationship. I cannot force a friendship or make someone go deeper than she wants to go. My prayer is that as I continue to pursue friendships, God will grant my desire for a close friend.

Melissa

When I lived in Nevada, God blessed me with a friendship with an amazingly gracious lady named Roxanne. I met her after her husband had a severe stroke. I wanted to help him have the best recovery possible. I barely knew either of them, but my heart was touched by the severity of his stroke and its consequences. I visited him in the hospital and in the rehab facilities and watched his progress.

Later, I went to their home and worked with him on physical exercises. I got to know Roxanne and see what a godly example she was to everyone who knew her.

While helping her move into a one-story home and doing simple chores, I watched her. I took lessons from her, though she never knew I was in her classroom. I watched how she expressed love to every person she met. She expressed her love aloud, in handwritten notes, through peanut butter cookies, and in prayer. I've never known a humbler or gentler person or seen Jesus's love on display in such clear ways. People were drawn to Roxanne. Each person she met thought they were her most cherished friend. They felt that way because that was how she made them feel. She was always looking for something good to praise.

I laugh when I recall the little things that I did to help her and how often she told me I was doing too much. The truth is, I needed to help her so I could be near her and so God could show me, by her example, how to love well. Roxanne gave me a picture of love in the flesh.

I eventually had to move away from this sweet friend. Now I'm in the business of following Roxanne's example. She was the gift I needed, and now I want to be that gift for others.

Kathi

My first friend has always been my mother. My father left her with three small children, so she struggled to do her best as a single mom. She worked very hard, and we never went without. She even found a way to pay for me to go to Girl Scouts and managed to send me to camp one year.

Still, I needed friends my own age, so I hung out with kids in my neighborhood. Every family on our street knew each other. My three girlfriends were Girl Scouts too. But as with most groups of girls, there was a pecking order. Julie and Michelle were the rich kids on the block. Shirley had a stay-at-home mom, and everyone on the block could go to her house if they needed help or lunch or a bandage for a skinned knee. I was the poor kid from a broken home.

This pecking order became a lifelong pattern.

Junior high is a blur to me. Somewhere between being a kid and entering my teens, I started drinking whiskey and Pepsi every day to fit in.

During high school, my mom moved us away to a different place, and I became hopeful that things would improve. I tried not to drink as much and to make friends. Instead, I became known as a drunk and a druggie. To the boys this meant I was easy, and to the girls this meant I was a slut, neither of which was true. More than anything in the world, I wanted to stay a virgin until I got married. Instead, I made friends with two girls, one of them talked me into meeting with some boys who were in their twenties, and I was raped.

I never had girlfriends after that. Not until I gave my life to the Lord and learned to trust Him with all my heart. I now have many sisters and brothers in Christ. For the first time, I am experiencing unconditional love from friends. We are like minded and know God has forgiven our sins and that we have eternal life with Him. We know He keeps His promises and will never let go of us. In His friendship circle, there is no pecking order. Amen.

Kristy

The first time I lost a best friend was when I was in third grade. My family lived in California, and I found out that my best friend and neighbor was moving to Chicago, Illinois. I remember being devastated and crying in my mother's lap.

She'd been raised by a mother who suffered from bipolar disorder, so she was uncomfortable with my out-of-control emotions.

Still, she tried to help me in her own way by having a going-away party for my friend. She made a cake in the shape of California and put it at one end of a long table and another cake, shaped like Illinois, at the other end. She put brown candles representing telephone poles down the center of the table between the two cakes. She stretched yarn from California up to the cardboard crossbars attached to the tops of the candles, to the other candle/telephone poles, and then down to the Chicago side of the cake. It still touches me to think of her using her creativity to help me deal with the loss of my best friend.

Unfortunately, though, that began a pattern of me having only one friend at a time. When that friend moved or changed, I was alone and had to find another friend. More recently, I lost my best friend (a former college roommate) to a long battle with multiple sclerosis. Even though her disease was continually progressing to the point of her being bedridden, on a feeding tube, and unable to speak, when she did pass away it was yet another devastating loss.

To this day, when I have a good friend, I worry about when something will happen to make that friend leave. It makes me afraid to develop new friendships. It seems like life would be easier if I had several friends. Then I would be less fearful of something happening to cause my one friend to leave. So now I am asking God to help me create a circle of trusted friends.

Doing It All for God
DAYS 17–20

For just as each of us has one body with many members, and these members do not all have the same function, so in Christ we, though many, form one body, and each member belongs to all the others. We have different gifts, according to the grace given to each of us. If your gift is prophesying, then prophesy in accordance with your faith; if it is serving, then serve; if it is teaching, then teach; if it is to encourage, then give encouragement; if it is giving, then give generously; if it is to lead, do it diligently; if it is to show mercy, do it cheerfully.

Romans 12:4–8

"Sheep bite."

That's what I heard at a leadership meeting over thirty years ago. I remember sitting there wondering why the pastor leading the meeting would say such a thing. As a new Christian brimming with zeal and exuberance for Christ, I found it deeply confusing. I was ready to feed the poor, save the lost, sacrifice time and energy for Jesus, and serve tirelessly. I couldn't wait to dive into the deep end of ministry. To feed His sheep.

Hadn't God called me to tend to His flock and those I hoped would join the fold? Now a pastor was telling me that sheep bit. What did he mean? What about all the "They'll know us by our love" I'd heard about and the joy of blessing others? Getting bit didn't sound very joyful.

I went ahead and served anyway, figuring that pastor must have been exaggerating based on one bad experience. I am a doer. I was blessed (or cursed!) with an abundance of energy. I walked at eight months old, and I haven't stopped since; and this predisposition applied at church. Good and bad, I said yes to a bevy of projects and pushed forward.

Then I started learning the meaning of the pastor's statement. Don't get me wrong; I loved serving in my church and worked alongside some incredible people. It blessed me to use my talents and areas of giftedness in ways that benefited others. I discovered that 90 percent of ministry was showing up. It wasn't about the big productions and programs. In fact, serving was more often about signing up to hold babies during a church service so their mommies could listen to a sermon or making time to talk with an elderly man who'd just lost his wife of sixty years. Ministry was about giving of my time and talents, whether noticeable or not, to serve God's people.

But I also discovered that, in the process of all this serving, God's sheep could and did bite me on occasion. Some gossiped, complained after I'd done my best, or went on the attack based on a misunderstanding. Others were downright divisive, caustic, or cruel. Each of these experiences hurt, but they also taught me a lot.

I learned the truth behind the expression "Hurt people hurt people." Ministry involves a lot of hurting people. In some cases, I didn't know a person was hurting until they bit me. In a few cases, I've done the biting without meaning to. This has taught me to see the most difficult people I encounter in ministry as walking wounded in need of a hospital. I've learned to remind myself that unkind words and hurtful behavior often has nothing to do with me. Still, these experiences left me worn out and discouraged at times. So I learned to be a good steward of my time, energy, and talents, and to be purposeful about who I poured myself into. Now when I do serve, I can do it with my whole heart and have space to recover when I get bitten. I learned the importance of constantly reminding myself Who I am really serving; whether I feel appreciated or not, I'm doing it for the Lord.

Ministry is exciting and fun, messy, and sometimes full of drama. But the blessings are worth the occasional bruises and bumps. Serving allows us to love as Christ loved, use our talents for His kingdom, and see what happens when His people come together for those in need, for the good of the community, or to encourage and edify one another.

When we focus on the blessings instead of every bite, we begin to see the beauty of God's plan for each of our unique gift. In His kingdom, each one is equally valuable and needed. I thank God for that!

Which gifts has God given you? How are you using them? Which ministries are you involved in? Are you still trying to find your place in the church, or are you in a new congregation? If that's the case, ask God to point you toward ministry opportunities. If you have been bitten by some of His sheep and are still recovering, ask Him to heal those wounds and restore your joy of serving.

Open your heart, mind, and life this week to how God might want to use you.

Day 17: Pray for ten minutes without interruption

God, I give You my acts of service today. Thank You for choosing to use me. Please help me to serve with joy even when it's difficult. Heal the wounds inflicted by others and help me to forgive. Lord, please provide new opportunities for me to serve, whether people see what I do or not. As I pray, fast, and sacrifice over the next few days, I want to submit my heart to You. Please show me my real motives in serving. Help me to minister and serve with a true heart of love for Your people. May I ultimately serve an audience of one—You. Amen.

Write down a few things that God reveals to you about ministry.
- o _____
- o _____
- o _____

Day 18: Fast/Sacrifice for twenty-four hours
Write down what God reveals to you during the fast.
- _____
- _____
- _____

Day 19: Identify
Write down any areas of ministry-related control, pride, bitterness, or hurt that God has put on your heart.
- _____
- _____
- _____

Day 20: Take action
What do you plan to do different regarding ministry and serving?
- _____
- _____
- _____

Doing It for God: Other Women's Stories

Rose

I have been to Mexico on many short-term mission trips to serve the local people. With each trip, I am always amazed by the results and the blessings. My mission is always to serve, and I help as much as I am able. Despite my age, those in charge always seems to find something for me to do. They include me as part of the team and treat me like an equal. I have even been able to be an example for the younger people. So I am a living example that the Lord can use us no matter what age we are.

One trip included building a house. I had never built a house before and didn't know anyone who was going on the trip, but I knew I needed to go. I'm so glad I did. What an experience! The work was hard, and I enjoyed every minute of it. One day I observed the work from the yard and saw all of God's people working together as a team, each doing their appointed tasks with peace and joy. I had never seen that before. They were working together to glorify God—and without any conflict. I was amazed! It was so heartwarming. It gave me a sense of peace. The moment when we all got to present the house to the family was so endearing that it's hard to describe I have been back three times since then and hope to go again.

I have also served in local projects, such as when my church did a 6K walk for water. This was another thing I'd never done before. I found a sponsor and started preparing by walking every day (even while recovering from bilateral hip bursitis). When the day came, I was determined to finish the race. I had to stop and rest many times, but I completed the walk in two hours. It was so delightful to come to the finish line and see a group of people I didn't know cheering me on.

"I can do all things through Christ who strengthens me"— including serve the Lord.

Amelia

I know God wants to use me, yet I often feel that I don't have much to give. How can I feel like this when I know He made me and created me to serve Him? Do I think He created me without any useful skills? If I really want to be His, why don't I find ways to serve Him?

I serve at church by being a greeter and helping with events, but beyond that, my tendency is to wait to be asked before I serve. If I find out that someone in my neighborhood has a need that I can help with, I do it. I mow lawns for some of my neighbors because I know they are working long hours and are tired or have new babies. I don't wait for them to ask for help; I just do it. So why not take the same approach at church?

Lord, open my eyes and heart to do what you want of me.

Recently, I found out about a yard cleanup for someone in the church who'd gotten injured. I drove by the woman's house and saw how out of control her yard was, and I'd never noticed. This taught me to open my eyes and try and find where the church needs me. God reminded me that I have more to give than I realize. After I got home, I went to the church office and told them I wanted to help with the yard cleanup.

My prayer is that I will continue to keep my eyes open for opportunities to serve instead of waiting to be asked. After all, if both of my eyes work, why not meet the needs that are right in front of me?

Lord, please show me what I can do to bring praise to You.

Mary

One of my favorite acts of service was delivering roses to women. They were always surprised to receive them, and I experienced the joy of seeing their beautiful smiles. That was one of my exciting opportunities to serve God in small but significant ways.

I also organized the food and music for funerals at my church, and in the process, experienced how good it felt to encourage and be there for the people who were hurting. Another time, I helped with a Valentine's Day banquet. It included music, a meal, a heart-shaped cake, and taking each couple's picture.

Each time I have the opportunity to serve, I'm reminded what a blessing it is to bless others.

Kristy

Several times in my life I have felt the Lord leading me to help others by providing a place for them to stay when they were struggling in life. This started in high school, when a friend of a friend needed a place to stay on weekend nights when her mother played in a band. Fortunately, my wonderful parents agreed when I offered our home. When I was in college but still living at home, I invited a friend to share my room when her home situation became too stressful for her. When I went away to college, I offered my room to my boyfriend's roommate's fiancée so she could work and plan their wedding after her family moved. That situation helped my parents as well, because she could watch my younger sister while my parents were at work.

Though these situations worked out well, I've learned the hard way that when I feel a nudge to help someone, I need to consider the other people involved—especially my family—and seek the Lord's wisdom and direction. I got into a pattern of letting empathy cloud my judgment and offering to help others without consulting my family or considering the consequences. Recently, for example, after inviting a friend's son to live with us, we ended up also making room for his girlfriend and her dog. They stayed on our property in an old, beat-up tent trailer.

Even though I felt the Lord leading us to provide for these young people, I feel like I really let my family down. This whole situation was hard on my husband, my son, and myself. I now see that I probably could have helped in other ways. As stressful as this experience was, it taught me that serving can (and should) include boundaries.

Bumps in the Road to Purpose
DAYS 21–24

Whatever you do, work at it with all your heart, as working for the Lord, not for human masters, since you know that you will receive an inheritance from the Lord as a reward. It is the Lord Christ you are serving.

Colossians 3:23–24

The first summer after my husband and I joined our church, we decided to participate in the family mission trip. It turned into a memory of a lifetime. But first we had to get there. Our "This cannot be happening" experience stands out in my memory as vividly as the joy of serving.

We departed early in the morning, towing our eleven-year-old twins, our eight-year-old daughter, and our youngest daughter, who was six at the time. We hit the highway ready for excitement, packed to the gills with gangly children, their emotional support stuffed animals, and the coveted portable video game system. We drove an old Suburban, which had been broken in through years of road trips, drink spills, and the assorted melted crayons that colored the cup holders. The roof was packed with suitcases, pillows, sleeping bags, and blankets, thanks to the newest addition to family vacations: an egg-shaped cargo carrier.

An hour into the trip, I glanced back at my children, watching their enthusiasm over our impending summer adventure. What a wonderful experience this would be for them, serving others and showing the love of Christ. I prayed that it would launch them into a life of ministry. Then I did a double take out the back window as the cars behind us started swerving around road debris. I gasped as one car almost sideswiped another in an attempt to avoid what looked like a pillow. Once that shock was over, I heaved a sigh of relief and thanked God that we'd dodged a near disaster before turning back around to ask my husband, "Did you see that? Someone lost a pillow back there."

To my right, I noticed a driver making exaggerated waving gestures and pointing toward the sky. What was she doing? I looked behind me again and almost leaped out of my seatbelt. I spotted a sleeping bag that looked just like my youngest daughter's. Then a familiar blanket disappeared under a truck's tire.

The cars behind us were dodging *our* things. Those were *our* sleeping bags, pillows, blankets, and clothes getting crushed on the California freeway, smashed like bugs on a windshield underneath the weight of hundreds of cars.

"Sam," I shouted to my husband. "The roof carrier is open!"

We pulled over in the next safe area to figure out what had happened. It didn't take long to determine that our cargo carrier had not been locked correctly. It had flown open, sending our belongings flying.

Most of our supplies lay in tatters on the freeway. All of our sleeping bags, gone. All of our pillows, gone. We couldn't retrieve any of it unless we wanted to get squashed too. We had two suitcases left, which thankfully held a lot of our clothes.

When Sam returned to the Suburban, he looked at me with a grimace on his face, shaking his head. "Do you know how much this trip already cost us? Now, we have to buy all new bedding and sleeping bags."

I could tell he felt deflated. He had been the one who forgot to lock the storage shell, causing our belongings to take flight like cotton balls in a tornado. The last thing he needed was for me to say, "I told you so." Our family mission trip was not starting out well. Rubbing my husband's nose in his mistake would not get us back on track.

I thought for a moment. We planned to spend that night at my parents' house. I patted Sam's arm. "Well, when we get to Mom and Dad's, we will borrow some bedding. I'm sure they won't mind."

We had no choice but to keep driving, thank God that no one got injured, and refuse to let this mishap ruin our trip.

Not only did we recover from this literal bump in the road, but I am convinced that we had a richer time because of it. After losing things that we could borrow and eventually replace, we spent a week serving people who didn't even have a proper home to live in. We experienced the blessing of helping to build a one-room house for them and see their tears of gratitude over receiving it. The moment of seeing our pillows and blankets scattered on the freeway paled in comparison to serving alongside our children. We didn't need to tell them, "See how blessed we are." They could see the evidence all around them.

The memory of this road trip to service reminds me that even the most exciting opportunities—whether it's a mission trip, a promotion, or a new home—include challenges. They can even fall through. We can either let those hiccups derail our joy, or we can move forward and consider how God might use both the good and the bad as part of His plan. What can we learn (besides "Next time, make sure the roof carrier is securely locked")? If nothing else, these experiences can teach us to surrender our desire for stress-free perfection.

What challenges are you facing in the midst of something good? Maybe God is asking you to surrender your expectations or to trust His grace after a mistake that set your goals back. Whatever He puts on your heart this week, savor each moment with Him as He works and restores your confidence in His plan.

Day 21: Pray for ten minutes without interruption

God, my days are Yours. Each shift I work, each person I serve, each new opportunity, even each mistake, is a chance for me to shine for You. Create divine appointments for me to share my faith in unique ways. I pray that You will protect me and remind me to make good decisions, especially when my actions impact those around me. Help me to trust Your grace when things don't go perfectly and to see mistakes as an opportunity to grow as a person. Lord, I give You today. Use me. Please help me serve You well, my Lord.

Write down a few things that God reveals to you as you pray.
- _____
- _____
- _____

Day 22: Fast/Sacrifice for twenty-four hours
Write down what God reveals to you during the fast.
- _____
- _____
- _____

Day 23: Identify
Write down some things that God wants you to surrender as you approach an upcoming opportunity.
- _____
- _____
- _____

Day 24: Take action
What do you plan you do differently now that you've spent this time with God?
- _____
- _____
- _____

Bumps in the Road to Purpose: Other Women's Stories

Rose

I was working the graveyard shift at a county facility in California. My husband was chronically ill, and my five sons were having a difficult time in school and at home. I had worked for about two years, and things were far from pleasant. I was frustrated at work and at home, trying to meet my family's needs, and I did not have any time for myself. I felt trapped, frustrated, angry, fearful, and depressed. I needed a change.

After a lot of thought, I finally decided to quit my stressful job. I was the main wage earner in my family, but I wouldn't be able to earn anything if stress made me sick. Within weeks, I found another position—one that I loved. It challenged me in good ways, and it allowed me to work during the day instead of at night. For the first time, I had a job I really enjoyed.

Even though it didn't last long, I look back on that experience as a time when I saw God meet a desperate need.

Rachel

I did not set out to be a teacher. I wanted to be a psychologist. After years of working to put myself through college, I chose teaching because I could earn my credential much sooner than I could become licensed as a psychologist. I'd had a career before this, but it had required a lot of travel. Teaching was much more conducive to being married and raising a family.

After completing my credential, I received two job offers in one day. I ended up working at an independent study charter school where some dear Christian friends also taught. I have been there for almost twenty years. In the early years, to be honest, it was only about doing my job, and I didn't engage much with my fellow teachers. But for the past five years, I have finally felt fulfilled. I've built strong connections with my students and coworkers. Those I work with all have different beliefs, but we get along well and have the same goal of servicing our students and families. I have become a coach, mentor, graduation coordinator, co-teacher for a writing class, and coordinator for testing. I am able to do all of this because I've been at the school for so many years and also because of the relationships with my administration and coworkers. As I look back at the changes, my decisions, and the twists and turns that my life has taken, I am all the more grateful for this teaching job.

Melissa

During my prayer time, God gave me a history lesson of my employment positions. Most of my jobs were simply that—jobs, as opposed to careers. They had some good points, but I never had a position I loved. I prayed about this frequently, especially when I was trapped in a miserable work environment because of financial need. Finally, I found the perfect place for me. When my husband accepted a job transfer and I had to leave, I cried. I had never done that before.

God graciously showed me that each one of these jobs—even the ones that tried me almost to the point of destruction—was a gift from Him for its season.

Now I am caught in a web of technology that is foreign to me. Everything is going online now, and I feel awkward and out of date using my devices. I require a lot of help, which makes me feel dumb. But I'm trusting that God will also use this, even if it's only to teach me some much-needed tech skills.

God has provided, and I have been blessed. He truly does more than we can ask or imagine. It has not been a straight or easy road. I recall tears and tantrums when uncertainty hit, but none of the fears behind those emotional moments became reality. God has been so good!

Amelia

When I was encouraged to run for president of a club I belonged to, I didn't want to do it. I enjoyed taking part in the club and what it had to offer, but I didn't feel like I had the skills for a leadership position. And I really didn't want to commit to what it would take to do the job. I resisted and resisted until the club got to the point where we might have to close down if we couldn't get people to fill the open leadership roles. So I accepted the role of club president and asked God to equip me with what I needed.

I took office in January 2020, then the COVID-19 pandemic hit in March. This club is for seniors, and many of our members had health issues that put them at risk. I wanted to protect them and stop meeting, but for many, this was their only chance to socialize. I was met with so much resistance that I finally agreed to open and close each meeting even though I wouldn't be attending because of COVID risks. I felt so defeated. God had equipped me to lead the group, but in this situation, I felt like I'd failed.

The next afternoon, the city issued orders that required the club to stop meeting in person. I was so thankful for the news. But I still questioned my ability to lead this group. One morning, while listening to the Christian radio station, I heard Matthew West's song "Do Something." It reminded me that if I just choose to let God use me, He can do anything. I needed to choose to open myself up, to hear Him, and be willing to follow His lead. I knew He was in control, so I needed to let go of *my* control and let Him be in charge.

I continue to trust. I know it isn't my job to understand what His plan is, and it isn't my job to make people do the wise thing, but it *is* my job to trust Him and His faithfulness to use me for His good.

Kristy

I have always struggled with a lack of confidence when it comes to my jobs. I think I am slow to work because I am afraid to make mistakes. I have noticed a pattern of constantly asking my coworkers questions.

When a coworker who knew the job thoroughly moved away, I was forced to rely on my knowledge to figure things out. We were so busy that we put off training before she left, then our office had to close due to the coronavirus pandemic.

God promised to work all things together for good. Through this forced shutdown of the office, He provided an easier transition for me. As we slowly reopened, I slowly learned my new responsibilities. I found myself praying constantly about my job, just as I did when I first started. This became a lesson in seeking the Lord and relying on Him daily as I learn to have confidence in the abilities that He equips me with.

Credit Cards, Cash, and My ATM
Days 25–28

"Bring the whole tithe into the storehouse, that there may be food in my house. Test me in this," says the Lord *Almighty, "and see if I will not throw open the floodgates of heaven and pour out so much blessing that there will not be room enough to store it."*
Malachi 3:10

While recovering from a disastrous marriage to a man who was so abusive that he tried to murder me, I cautiously entered into a new relationship. Sam was different from any man I'd ever dated. He was grounded in Christ and showed me his faith through actions, not just words. Still, when he asked me to marry him, I panicked. It wasn't that I didn't want to marry him. I did. I loved Sam. But in addition to being emotionally destroyed by my first marriage, those years with an abusive man had left me financially devastated as well. After narrowly escaping, I'd filed bankruptcy. In fact, I'd had to file twice in the ten years between when we married and when I left. Now, at thirty years old, although I had a great job working for a Fortune 50 company, did my best to be financially responsible, and didn't have any debt (because bankruptcy erased it), I didn't have any extra money and had horrible credit.

Sam knew about my elopement at twenty years old, the ten years of domination and domestic abuse, and the moment when I had to flee for my life. I'd never had a reason to tell him about the bankruptcy part until now. How would he respond when he found out? My parents wouldn't be helping with the wedding, and I had no way to pay for the event.

I finally found the courage to share everything with Sam. My financial mess did not stop him from wanting to marry me. He loved *me*, not my money (or lack of). We just had to figure out how to pay for the wedding.

I'd eloped with my first husband. Sam had never been married. So neither of us had ever had a wedding. The minute we told his parents about our engagement, they got excited and started helping us plan a summer wedding on the lawns of their riverfront estate.

We did what every normal American couple would do. We put our entire wedding and honeymoon on plastic. In the end, we put $20,000 on credit cards!

Soon into our marriage, we tried to start a family. After numerous emotional letdowns, we started fertility treatments. When they worked, we were elated. But at thirty one weeks, I went into preterm labor and delivered my twins, one weighing two pounds and the other weighing three. They spent two months in the NICU. We added those lovely medical bills to a wedding on credit and continued sending minimum payments. The stress began to build. We had two babies at home, one on a heart monitor. I was working full time, so we hired a live-in babysitter. All of this added up to a pile of monthly bills that we could barely cover.

We got the miracle we needed when our church offered a financial class taught by the late Larry Burkett, who was a predecessor of Dave Ramsey. The class taught a simple budgeting plan with the following priorities: tithe, taxes, bills, save. Larry's plan promised to get most people out of debt in eighteen months. We signed up and went all in. We developed a spreadsheet, tightened our belts, took what few dollars we had left each month, and applied that money to our smallest bills. Once those were paid, we took that extra money and applied it to the next highest bill. As promised, we were debt-free in less than eighteen months.

This system changed how we managed our money.

One thing we always did was tithe. There were times when we couldn't afford to go on dates, eat out, or buy new things, but we were not going to rob God. As the Creator and the giver of all, He asks us to test Him on this, promising to bless us and open the floodgates. We understood that His promise was not an insurance plan (as in, we tithe and bingo—God gives).

Other passages, such as the Genesis account of Cain and Abel, reminded us that God looks at the heart. But this experience taught me that if we set up our finances in the correct way and are good stewards of what we have been given, and if we give to God first, we will have what we need and be blessed.

This continues to be true. It can be true for you too.

What is it about money that we find especially difficult to surrender? No matter what your financial situation looks like right now, I encourage you to release it to God this week. Ask Him to show you how to be an even better steward of what He provides. If you carry fears related to money, ask Him to help you trust Him more and recognize His provisions. Pay special attention to the freedom that comes when you trust God with your money.

Day 25: Pray for ten minutes without interruption

My Lord, Your Word says You own the cattle on a thousand hills. Everything I have is Yours. It is all to Your glory that I am allowed the smallest of possessions. I thank You for what You have entrusted to me. Help me to see and release my struggle with money, credit, covetousness, or foolish financial behaviors. The deepest prayer of my heart is for wisdom to use whatever You give me for Your glory. Please reveal areas where I am enslaved by money or lack common sense in how I deal with it. Help me to be obedient to tithe and give generously to Your works. Thank you for all the ways You have blessed me, Lord. Amen.

Write down a few things that God reveals to you about finances.

-
-
-

Day 26: Fast/Sacrifice for twenty-four hours

Write down what God reveals to you during the fast.

-
-
-

Day 27: Identify

Write down the areas of money-related control or fear that you have identified.

-
-
-

Day 28: Take action

What do you plan to do differently now that you know what needs to change?

-
-
-

Credit Cards, Cash, and My ATM: Other Women's Stories

Rose

When I was in grade school, my brothers and I got $1 a week for lunches. I chose to make my own lunch and save my money for things I wanted to buy later. My family was very poor, so this taught me to save at a very early age.

But financial struggles still followed me through life. When my husband left me and my income was cut in half, I desperately needed a reliable car. I was also saving for two exciting trips. I wanted to pay cash for the car. I looked and prayed and was specific about what I wanted. After many disappointments, I started getting frustrated. Then a friend recommended a dealer. I passed the place on my way home from work, and the Lord nudged me to stop. The dealer had four cars that met my requirements and price range. The car I left with became known as my God car. It was not only an answer to prayer, but it was a concrete reminder of God's goodness.

Rachel

While I was growing up, money always seemed to bring stress. I often heard my parents talking about the lack of money, or my dad trying to figure out ways to earn more. My siblings and I were encouraged to tithe at Sunday school, but I never saw my parents tithe. They also never spent money on themselves, and I saw them give generously to others.

When my father passed away suddenly, I discovered a lot of credit card debt that he'd kept hidden from my mom. This was overwhelming for me. While grieving, I had to be strong for my mom and help her deal with the reality that she would lose her home and needed to learn how to manage her money.

Because of this, I never liked having a credit card balance. I used cash and felt guilty if I bought something I didn't need. Like my parents, I was generous with my giving to others but never tithed regularly. Then I met my husband, who was very firm on tithing, and we made a discipline to always give to God first.

But outside of tithing, my husband didn't manage money well, so we decided that I would take care of the finances. That was how I found out about his huge business loan debt. Once again, money equaled stress. He struggled to get and keep jobs due to his lack of education, so I became the primary breadwinner.

My husband is a good man and hates that I must carry such a burden. I must admit that I desperately wanted and still want to feel taken care of by someone. Through all this, we continue to tithe. We believe we are doing what is right and continue to lead with an open hand. When I start to feel anxious about money, I remind myself that fear is not from the Lord.

Money is something that God continually works on with me. Not the managing and budgeting part, because I have that down. Our work is focused on my learning to trust Him to provide no matter the situation.

Melissa

When I was a teenager, my babysitting money (thirty-five cents per hour) was all mine. My paper route money was also mine. That was how I bought my pink Schwinn bicycle in sixth grade—the rusty one that still sits in my garage.

The money I made as a bank teller went toward college expenses. My teaching money paid for an apartment, a car, groceries, clothes, and my wedding. From all that money, I gave a tiny gift to the Lord. I am so ashamed of my selfishness as I reflect on that now. My parents always gave money to the church. I remember them discussing it as

I grew up. My dad was diligent about his finances. He even led church giving campaigns.

After I married and my husband accepted Christ, we began to seriously evaluate our giving to the Lord. We made tithing a priority. It was a huge step of faith, which we grew into as we inched up our giving over several years. In the process, we discovered that we couldn't out-give God. Everything we gave came back to us in some unexpected way. Eventually, we moved beyond the tithe to giving heart gifts to the Lord, giving to others in need, and contributing to multiple charities. We have never looked back.

Throughout this study, God continually brings me back to thanksgiving. All the prayers, all the fasting, and all the reflecting have shown me a God who has been faithful beyond my expectations.

At one point, Jacob and I had two kids in college and one in grad school, a mortgage, two car payments, and car insurance for young drivers. One of our daughters became engaged, so then we had a wedding as well. Since the engaged couple was still in college, we agreed to help them reach graduation by continuing some financial support, provided they also got jobs. Once they began senior year they decided, unbeknownst to us, to report to the financial aid office. They filled out paperwork for financial assistance. Imagine our surprise and delight when they called to say they had received grants to complete their last year of schooling. This was a blessing none of us anticipated. We still thank God for it.

Age changes one's perspective on almost everything, including money. I have found that I don't pay a lot of attention to money anymore, except for what is required. Why worry about it when I know I'll always have what I need? Right now, my husband and I donate to a hospital that has been struggling with the COVID-19 pandemic. Everyone I know is experiencing financial distress and trauma. But Jacob and I continue trusting God to show us how we can help and glorify Him with our money.

Amelia

While picking up supplies for a spaghetti dinner fundraiser, I got in a car accident. I wasn't injured, but my old car was totaled. A relative allowed me to borrow a car for a week, but I had no idea what I would do after that.

On the night of the fundraiser, thirty minutes before the event started, I was alone in the storage room with a member of the planning team when she collapsed and had a massive stroke. I caught her and shouted for someone to call 911. Someone else called the woman's family. All I could do after that was pray for her. On the way home, I had to return my borrowed car and figure out how I would get around with just my bike and public transportation.

The next day I got a call from a family member of the woman who's had the stroke. They had heard about my accident and asked me if they could keep the woman's car at my house while she recovered. "Feel free to use it," they said.

"That's what she would want."

I was shocked and thankful. I knew God's hand was in this.

After the woman was discharged from the hospital, I used the car to help the family care for her. Six weeks later, the woman was admitted to the hospital again. I had a chance to pray with her in a moment when she felt afraid and knew she was dying. She suddenly changed her mood, turned to me, and told me the car was mine. She even told her family, "The car is hers." Five days later, she went home to be with God.

This car was fourteen years newer than the one I lost and nicer than anything I could ever afford. Every time I get in it, I remember His provision and ability to bless us beyond our dreams.

Jeanine

Minimum-wage spousal support. I was going through a divorce and in mediation with my pro bono attorney when I first heard the term. As a stay-at-home mom and primary caregiver for my daughter, I had assumed I would be entitled to both child and spousal support, at least until I got back on my feet. I'd walked into that mediation with only custody on my mind, wanting to keep my daughter safe and on a schedule that was good for her. With my focus on that and not wanting to break down crying in front of my ex, I didn't realize that I was answering all the financial questions wrong. My answers had proven that I could earn more than minimum wage, so in addition to being responsible for $7,000 worth of debt, I would not receive spousal support.

I sat in my car and cried. How would I care for my daughter?

My first financial miracle came a week later. A former coworker contacted me and offered me a job. That allowed me to slowly begin to catch up. As I regained my confidence, I was able to branch out to a different job that allowed me to work from home and grow in my skills. I will never forget how freeing it felt when I got a raise and finally paid off the debt to my ex-husband. I was completely free of him financially.

When I consider all the valuable things I learned through this experience, I wouldn't change a thing. I firmly believe that God orchestrated this plan, knowing the trials and tribulations would make me stronger.

Kristy

My husband worked in construction management in the banking industry, but when development slowed down and construction loan divisions were phased out, he got laid off. This happened at multiple companies. In the meantime, both of his parents and two of his brothers passed away in a short time period. After so much loss and unemployment, he was diagnosed with depression.

We had used all of our savings and 401(k) funds, and we were paying for COBRA insurance, which we needed for preexisting conditions. We were in danger of losing our home. Through all of this, we tried to tithe and trust the Lord. I knew I needed to find a job but had no idea where to start. Despite my lack of skills and experience, the Lord led me to an opportunity to work part time for a local doctor. When things slowed down there and my hours got cut, God sent a temporary job that turned into a full-time position. Eventually, my husband got the help he needed and started working full time again as well.

Now that we are on the other side of that season of stress, I am trying to surrender to God every day, not just when we are struggling.

Days 29–32

The man said, "The woman you put here with me—she gave me some fruit from the tree, and I ate it." Then the LORD God said to the woman, "What is this you have done?" The woman said, "The serpent deceived me, and I ate."

Genesis 3:12–13

Growing up in Southern California with its long, hot summers, my siblings and friends and I spent our days playing in the many fields in our neighborhood. They were filled with acres of dry grass, but to us they were the perfect playground. I admit that as a preteen, I had a bit of a fascination with fire. I loved to play with matches and burn just about anything that would ignite. Whenever my family had a campfire or bonfire, I observed wide eyed as my father lit and stoked them. I loved the sulfur smell and watching the blue flames dance over the coals. Don't worry; this obsession did not last into adulthood. While lighting candles for a romantic dinner, I don't look for something else to set ablaze. I grew out of savoring the fragrance of smoke and ash. But at its peak, this youthful curiosity almost got me into big trouble.

One particularly scorching summer day, when I was about nine years old, my friends and I were playing in one of our favorite local fields. We were doing what kids do—goofing off—and trying to improve on our tree house, which was missing a few key wooden steps. I came prepared, as any young girl of nine would, with a hammer and a book of matches. I stood back as the group began nailing new steps to the huge tree we'd claimed. I gazed intently at the shiny flax-colored clumps of dry brush in the field. Then I lit a match. Again, I eyed the brush. The intoxicating smoke floated to my nostrils. *Mmm*. How would it smell combined with dry grass? I had to know! I threw the flaming match down onto the cluster of fuel. It burned bright for a second, then a small gust of wind blew out the flame, leaving only the scent of fire and a trace of black smoke. *That was so cool!* If one match created that much fun, what would another do?

Swoosh went the match against the cardboard. Down went my match into the weeds.

Up went the satisfying little flame. Up went the poof of smoke. *Yes!*

But within just a few short seconds, three-foot-high flames had spread and started to swallow up the field.

My satisfaction turned to fear. I screamed. What had I done? My friends frantically went into firefighter mode, searching for water to douse the quickly consuming flames.

One of the kids pointed to a familiar house. "They have a pool!"

We ran across the street to our friend's house, barged through the back fence, grabbed their hose, and filled their small kiddie pool with water.

"Hurry!" I shouted.

We rushed back to the field, only to have all that water slosh out as our young legs ran toward the edge of what was now a huge and dangerous fire.

An adult neighbor, looking down from a two-story window, saw the commotion and yelled at us, "You kids had better stick around. I just called the fire department."

I did what most nine-year-old children would do in that situation. I ran away as fast as I could! My friends followed.

That night, my parents and siblings and I were eating dinner. Our topics of conversation covered the typical family news. My father led the discussion, eager to know how his lovely wife and perfect children had filled that hot summer day.

"So, what did you kids do?"

I squirmed in my chair and took a drink of my milk. I looked around. My stomach churned with dread over how my dad would react when he found out what I had done with *my* afternoon. I didn't even want to think about what my punishment would be. My brothers started talking about their afternoons. I waited for Dad to ask, "What about you, Jeanette?" He didn't. I breathed a sigh of relief. Nobody was looking at me. I was off the hook. That is, until my oldest brother, Joe, offered up some local news of the day.

"Hey, you know that field over by the grocery store? Well, it burned up today. There were fire trucks and police cars everywhere. The whole field went up like a tinderbox." Then he added. "They said some girl started it."

Mom's jaw dropped open with shock. "What was that child thinking?"

"Which girl was it?" Dad asked.

I bit my lip. My brother probably couldn't wait to rat me out. "Some girl named Jennie."

My little brother Tommy looked at me. I tried to act nonchalant, thinking, *Jennie? They know, they know.* I was in the biggest trouble of my life! They knew!

As a kid my nickname was Jeanie, not Jennie. They didn't get my name right. But it was close enough.

My dad turned to my brother and asked him a few more questions. "Jennie, huh? I don't recall a family in the neighborhood with a daughter named Jennie. Did they say how old she was?"

My older brother shook his head. "They didn't say."

I sat quietly pushing my peas across my plate, trying to look innocent. "I don't know a Jennie."

Within seconds, the conversation moved to swimming and our summer garden. My family forgot all about the neighborhood disaster story. I was completely off the hook. Not caught! The fire story remained a secret for years, until as an adult I finally confessed the folly to my parents. They barely remembered the incident and actually laughed at my story of running with the kiddie pool to douse the blaze.

But between the time I started that fire and the time I confessed my guilt, I had a secret. An invisible wedge existed between my parents and me. There was also a wedge between God and me. I'd prayed during the fire and many times after, but not once had I asked God for forgiveness or taken responsibility for my careless action.

It disturbs me to recall myself back then, so pleased to realize that everyone thought another girl started the fire. What if we'd had a Jennie in our neighborhood and she'd been falsely accused? Would I have let her pay the price for my crime to avoid getting in trouble, continuing to let my family think the fire wasn't my fault?

I could have done more than just burn a field of dry grass that day. I could have damaged property, injured someone, or even taken a life.

But I wasn't the first girl to hide from my sin or try to blame someone else. When Eve ate the forbidden fruit, she blamed the serpent, and Adam blamed Eve. That set the path for sinful man, who is often so quick to blame someone or something else for missteps, carelessness, and deliberate sin.

Let's face it, it's hard to take responsibility when we've messed up or when the same thing old thing trips us up again and again. But doing so is not only an act of obedience to God, it is a sign of maturity and spiritual growth. Confessing may lead to consequences, but we have a clear conscience and a pure heart before God.

Are you carrying the weight of an unconfessed sin or a destructive habit or pattern? What excuses have you made? What is holding you back from confessing what you did or admitting you have a problem?

This week, allow God to reveal any sins or ungodly patterns that need to be brought into the light. Surrender your fear, shame, and any possible consequences to Him. Let Him cleanse your heart so you can experience His freedom.

Day 29: Pray for ten minutes without interruption

Lord, since my youth I've hidden from You. I've failed to reveal my missteps, my sin. I've blamed others and shirked the responsibility of my actions. Heavenly Father, I earnestly seek Your face. I give You permission to search my heart and reveal the errors of my ways. Show me what I am doing that puts a wedge between me and others and You. Help me to be repulsed by any half-truth and disgusted by my actions when they displease You. I love You, my God, and pray that You will guide me. Help me to establish a new, bold, and mature way of life for You. I pray this in Your name. Amen.

Write down what God puts on your heart to confess.
- _____
- _____
- _____

Day 30: Fast/Sacrifice for twenty-four hours
Write down what God reveals to you during the fast.
- _____
- _____
- _____

Day 31: Identify
Write down any area where you've tried to justify sin.
- _____
- _____
- _____

Day 32: Take action
What do you plan to do differently now that you have a pure heart before God?
- _____
- _____
- _____

Not My Fault: Other Women's Stories

Rose

My husband and I were living in a rural area. It was very hot and dry. My husband was at work and I was alone. We had a burn barrel on one side of the house. It was filled with trash. I decided to light it without thinking about the results. The fire spread beyond the can and reached the dry grass. I got the hose but couldn't contain the fire. I was terrified: What if it burned down our house, or the neighbor's house, and everything around it?

I finally got it together enough to call the fire department, and they put out the fire. I was too frightened to take responsibility for my part in the emergency, so I lied to the fire department about how it happened. I'm sure they knew I had started it. The firemen left me with my lie. I never told my husband the truth. I never asked God for forgiveness until now. Now I am experiencing the relief of having a clean conscience.

Melissa

I recall a time when my husband and I were on the verge of divorce. It was a truly dark situation. I could only see his blame in it. So could he. It nearly killed us.

We had dated for several years before getting married and never had a fight. He was quiet and gentlemanly. In fact, he was my white knight in shining armor. My friends were jealous of our relationship. However, underneath the shining armor, Jacob had some stored-up anger. During our engagement period, we had a major falling out. I let him accept all the blame for it, and we got married as planned.

But we had a lot of unresolved issues. We should have had Christian counseling, but we weren't wise enough to seek help.

During the most difficult point in our marriage, God allowed me to see my part in the problem. In His kindness, He revealed the truth over time, in small pieces that I could handle. I began to see my pattern of blaming all of our issues on Jacob instead of taking responsibility for my own shortcomings. I finally talked to Jacob, but I have learned that healing takes time. We must live with the consequences of our choices. For example, I was the one who accepted the engagement proposal knowing he was prone to anger, and I was the one who went through with the wedding when, looking back, I probably should have called it off.

Once we became believers, we had new hope. As followers of Christ, we have a Counselor at no charge in the Holy Spirit, and God has been our healer. He has changed me and challenged me to examine my own heart's motives. It's not simple, and it's not something I enjoy, but it has truly been a great help to me.

God has used this situation to help us become more holy. Through this study, God showed me one more piece of this crazy puzzle. Without this big boulder of a problem in our path, I'm not certain my husband and I would have become believers. For that reason, I wouldn't erase its pain. Once, while reading Joel in the Bible, I was struck by God's promise to the Israelites: "I will restore the years the locusts have eaten." That verse has become a key promise for me. I am now watching it be fulfilled in my personal life.

Kathi

It was their fault: my mom and dad's. Why did they have three children when they hated each other so much? It was their fault we were poor. It was their fault I went to bad schools, and it was their fault I could never go to college. It was their fault I drank. It was their fault I got raped. It was their fault my marriage failed.

This was my mindset for a long time.

I now know that I made some choices too. I was desperate for love but didn't love myself. I turned away from God. When He tried to reach me, I was so angry at the people who hurt me that I didn't let Him in. I know God has been trying to help me for a long time. I am ashamed of how long. But God doesn't see time the way I do. He just sees right now.

"Now that you have purified yourselves by obeying the truth so that you have sincere love for each other, love one another deeply, from the heart. For you have been born again, not of perishable seed, but of imperishable, through the living and enduring word of God" (1 Peter 1:22–23).

I finally reached a point where I knew I had to stop letting what my mom and dad did define my life. I had to let go and let God change me. But I had to work for it. I had to learn what and who God is.

"Do not merely listen to the word, and so deceive yourselves. Do what it says" (James 1:22).

Now I enjoy opening the Bible to randomly see what God has to say to me. It's often right on the mark of what I'm feeling. This teaches me to rely on Him, not others. Being weak doesn't mean I lack faith. I am strong because I have the strength of the Lord by His grace and for His glory. Amen.

Me and My Plate
DAYS 33–36

Do you not know that your body is a temple of the Holy Spirit who is in you, whom you have received from God? You are not your own; you were bought at a price. Therefore, glorify God with your body.

1 Corinthians 6:19–20

My mother used to call me Skinny Annice when I was a kid. I never thought much about it at the time, but I was definitely thin and lanky. I was a squirrely girl with way too much energy for activities that required sitting still. I danced around so much that my brother used to tease me and call me a fairy.

My upbringing also included plenty of food. My parents were first-generation Italian Americans, so we ate a lot of pasta, vegetables, and fruit. I would say it was a pretty healthy Mediterranean diet before that was considered a thing. I don't remember ever being hungry. I do remember eating ice cream, and at times, lots of ice cream. I can still picture my mother taking me to downtown Panorama City, me perched up on the soda fountain counter at Woolworths, wide eyed in anticipation, as a huge hot fudge sundae with whipped cream and a cherry was placed in front of my seven-year-old body. Pure heaven! I didn't have to consider the calories. What kid does? As soon as I got home, I would work the sundae off without knowing I was doing it. I rode my bike without stopping, sometimes for miles. I played street baseball and hide and seek with my siblings and the neighbor kids until it was dark, swung on swings, and swam in the pool until I looked like a wrinkled prune.

Such was my personal health and diet plan as a child.

In high school, I was on the drill team and a small precision group that many schools now call drum line. I joined the gymnastics team and the cheer squad. I also played powderpuff football and ran several miles a week just because I wanted to. So I was fit. I thought nothing of consuming thousands of calories a day. I pretty much ate whatever I wanted, whenever I wanted to eat.

Then came college. I was ready to tackle the world. I registered for nineteen units, found a small apartment close to school, and landed a waitress job at the local coffee shop. My personal fitness and high activity level came to an abrupt halt as the mound of books kept me sitting and studying. Eating became a fun and mindless activity that helped get the next chapter review completed and memorization cards created. One fantastic benefit of working at the restaurant was the discount on meals. I was allowed two meals for each shift I worked, and the company deducted a few dollars from my paycheck for them. They deducted the same amount no matter what I ordered, so I could have whatever I wanted. Since I paid for my own food at home, and the restaurant deducted money from my check automatically, I most certainly wanted to get my money's worth when I worked.

My routine was always the same: I went in early for my shift, had a full meal of chicken fried steak, mashed potatoes, corn and gravy, soup, salad, and dessert. But wait, there's more! After my shift ended at midnight, I did it again. I ordered a bacon cheeseburger, fries, a shake, and chocolate cake à la mode. My uniforms started feeling tight, but I honestly didn't take notice. I just chose baggier clothes to wear the rest of the time, and off I went.

Later in the year, I needed a physical for school. Of course, the exam included getting weighed. Because I'd always been skinny and never had a reason to dread the scale, I jumped right on. No biggie.

Then the doctor asked me, "Are you feeling okay? Is everything going well at school?" I told him, "Yes. Why?"

He gently informed me, "You've gained quite a bit of weight since your last appointment. If you keep gaining like you did this year, you'll be at an unhealthy weight in no time."

He told me how much I'd gained, and what I could expect to weigh at this time next year if the pattern continued. He used words like *obesity*. How was that possible? I'd weighed the same since I finished growing. Maybe a little more at certain times, but not much more, and I always went back to my usual weight quickly. His "if you keep this up" warning number shocked me. I sat there fighting tears as I looked down at the roll around my stomach. I had more than a small muffin top. How long had that been there?

That's when I realized I hadn't just gained the freshman fifteen; I'd gained a freshman forty! When it finally sank in that I was not a size 7/8 anymore, I started to buy over-the-counter diet pills in hopes that a miracle drug would help me melt forty pounds in a week. I went from diet to diet, eating poorly and not really exercising at all.

As the year progressed, I managed to lose about ten pounds. I still had quite a bit to go. Then I heard some very good advice: don't diet, change your lifestyle. (I know, so profound!) The recommendation included three easy guidelines:

1. Put half as much as you usually would on your plate.
2. Put your fork down between bites, and always sit when you eat.
3. Use a small salad plate for meals, not a dinner plate.

If I wanted ice cream, I planned to eat a smaller dinner and make that my treat for the day. If I had a high-calorie drink, I ate a lower calorie nutritious lunch.

I adopted the 80/20 diet: eat 80 percent healthy food each day and 20 percent whatever I wanted, and stick to a set number of calories. This method also stressed the importance of being active every day.

As a believer, I realized that God had created my body. His Spirit lived in me. Not only did I want to lose weight and stay healthy for myself, but I wanted to do it for Him as well.

The Scripture for this section of our 40 Days of Surrender says that we were bought at a price. Jesus gave His life for us. He gave us eternal salvation, and we are not our own. Therefore, we are told to glorify God with our bodies. It is one of the many ways we can honor Him. God doesn't ask us to starve ourselves to lose weight or take diet pills until we are shaky. He doesn't even require us to aim for a certain number on the scale or a certain size. That's how eating disorders are developed, and not all of us were created to be slim. Our goal is to do our best to live a healthy lifestyle and care for the bodies He gave us. Sometimes this means changing our eating habits, exercising more, or both. And sometimes it means surrendering to the body God gave us and caring for it even if we'll never look like a model.

How would you describe your physical health right now? As you consider God's desire for you to be healthy and the Bible's words about honoring Him with your body, how can you better care for yourself? Do you need to add a few carrots to your diet, switch soda with more water, or limit fast food? Do you need to exercise more or find a walking partner for motivation and accountability? Or are you one of the women who has knocked herself out trying to fit into a certain mold, and now you need to honor God by accepting the body type He gave you and focus on health instead of the numbers on your scale?

The wonderful part of a moment like this is that it's between you and God, not you and me or you and your skinniest friend. So what do you sense God telling you about your health right now? Invite Him to be your health coach over the next few days.

Day 33: Pray for ten minutes without interruption

Lord, I give You my body. Your Word tells me You want me to glorify You with it, but I confess, I don't always do that. God, help me. Help me to make good choices in what I put into my body. I ask You to please allow me to crave the foods that my body needs and to resist the foods that will harm me. When I have the choice to exercise or not, fill me with the desire to get up and move. Draw me to the healthier lifestyle that You desire for me. I ask for Your help in creating a body that can give You glory. Amen.

Write down a few things that God reveals to you as you pray.
- _____
- _____
- _____

Day 34: Fast/Sacrifice for twenty-four hours
Write down what God reveals to you during the fast.
- _____
- _____
- _____

Day 35: Identify
Write down what God is teaching you about your body image, diet patterns, and overall physical health.
- _____
- _____
- _____

Day 36: Take action
What do you plan to do now that you know what needs to change?
- _____
- _____
- _____

Me and My Plate: Other Women's Stories

Sheila

Food was a comfort for me—a temporary stress reliever. For me, eating was almost as soothing as visiting one of my favorite places: the mountains, sitting in the forest next to a waterfall just embracing the sounds of the water flowing, the breeze rustling in the trees, animals scurrying around and birds singing, soaking up the peace of nature with the world and my troubles far behind. Because of this, my weight went up and down. I had my overweight wardrobe, clothes that were tight, and outfits I wanted to fit into someday. I was always on the hunt for a quick-fix diet, but I didn't want to pay for a gym membership and have other people watch me work out. It was an endless cycle.

Then, after fifteen years of marriage, I found myself facing a divorce. I was in overwhelming emotional pain with two kids to care for. All I wanted to do was curl up in the corner of a room and give up, but I couldn't. In order to protect my kids from my tears, I started taking walks near the house after putting them to bed. That was where I cried, yelled, and poured out my heart. Sometimes walking almost turned to running as I released all of my pain and worries to God. After that, I could go on and face tomorrow. Soon I started to crave my walks and talks with the Lord. They got me through my divorce. Without trying to, I lost weight and improved my overall health.

After I'd raised my kids and found a wonderful second husband, I became a Body & Soul Fitness instructor. I was fifty years old and had severe stage fright, but I wanted other women to benefit from the healthy choices that I'd learned to make. As a group fitness instructor, I learned that exercise is great therapy—that it helps us physically, mentally, emotionally, and spiritually. Mind, body, and soul.

I now recognize that after adding exercise into my routine, I was more conscious about what I ate, when I ate, and why I was eating. My mood and self-esteem improved, I was better equipped to handle stress, and I slept better. My conscious contact with the Lord increased as I combined my exercise time with prayer and listening to Him.

I still revert to bad habits sometimes when dealing with stress and anxiety, but God is not done with me yet. He has a plan to grow me, use me, and send me to places that blow my mind as I trust Him with my life more and more.

Melissa

I'm one of those rare-breed women who has never belonged to a gym. Since having a painful episode of sciatica in 1996, I have continued to do the daily therapy exercises I learned. They take about forty-five or fifty minutes each morning, but I never skip them. I feel that being committed to this routine has helped me avoid repeat episodes. When I developed knee problems, I had to add a few new moves to the morning routine. Sometimes I hate the time devoted to this, but I see it as essential for my physical health.

I have been a lifetime member of WW (formerly Weight Watchers) since the last millennium. I am fairly disciplined about what I eat. In fact, I've never had a single doughnut on a Sunday morning. I stay away from the café. I don't even like coffee—not even the smell. Yeah, I really am weird.

My besetting food issues are sugar and crunchy things. I especially love popcorn and tortilla chips. But sugar is an absolute stumbling block. God and I have gone over this issue many times. I can eliminate it for a season, until a celebration comes along, and I get addicted to sugar again. I have struggled with this a lot during the pandemic, finding that I want to turn to comfort food. The days of fasting for 40 Days of Surrender have helped keep that monster at bay. God gave me a verse years ago to help me: "Keep your servant also from willful sins; may they not rule over me. Then I will be blameless, innocent of great transgression" (Psalm 19:13). When I think of overeating treats, desserts, or sugary foods, I consider that too much is what God's Word calls a willful sin. My body belongs to God. Remembering this is helpful, but at times it fades into the back of my mind, or I choose to ignore it.

While doing this study, I am actually enjoying the fasting days. Sometimes I feel they come a bit too close together, but once the fast begins, the time is meaningful. God has helped me identify my need to conquer the sugar habit. This is something I can only do with His help.

Today I did not eat any dark chocolate peanut M&Ms. They are my normal daily treat. I did not have any cookies, candy, desserts, or sweets of any kind. If I could do this once a week, it would feel like progress. I am determined to do it. With God's help, once a week could morph into twice a week.

Last night I awoke at about 4:00 a.m. I was awake enough to talk to God for an hour before getting up. It was a most remarkable encounter with Him, and I'm still in awe of the gift He gave me. In that early morning hour, he healed a deep wound. Later, He helped me understand how my personal body image has controlled my life.

I have had a bad image of my appearance since childhood. My mom sewed most of my clothes when I was in elementary school. When I was around eleven, I was being measured for a dress. Mom said, "You have no waist." Just as she was saying, "You have no hips either," my brother walked through the kitchen and made a negative comment about my body. Obviously, I have never forgotten this. To my brother, it was a silly joke. I knew that at the time, but it affirmed what I'd already thought about myself.

Most of my life I have been trying to change myself into what I would define as "perfect, or at least pretty." Well, my efforts haven't worked. I've realized that by doing this I was insulting my Creator, God, who designed me to look and be unique. When I look at nature, which is phenomenally beautiful, I see that none of it is uniform, symmetrical, or without quirks. These are the marks of character. Since considering that, I have become more accepting of my body. Having said this, I am looking forward to heaven and my new body.

Amelia

Sugar... oh, the sweet taste of sugar. One taste is never enough. I think I am letting sugar become a real problem. I can't stop at eating one bite of a cookie, or even one cookie. On many occasions "I'll only have one" has turned into me eating the whole box. I have to admit that I am giving my control over to sugar. It has been a problem for as long as I can remember.

I have been heavy since I was a kid. I came from a "large-boned" family, and we all accepted the way we looked. I had been taught that God made each of us different, and we are all His beautiful creations. I took that to include my weight.

Last year, after over fifty years of drinking soda, I decided to give it up. This was a huge challenge for me. Mom loved soda too, and we always had soda in the house, first regular then diet. The diet soda became an addiction. I couldn't go more than a couple of hours without one. I knew I had to quit, and to do that, I had to go cold turkey. I replaced it with water or an occasional iced tea. At first, each day without my diet soda was a huge challenge for me. But I finally did it.

Now I find myself asking, "Is there something else that has control over me?" I think there is. It is my sweet tooth. It was a magic food when I was growing up. Something sweet could make everything better. Now I have to admit that sugar has control of me. How can I change that? I know I have to give God control of my life, but that means I have to work on my lack of control.

I know God's love is pure and will satisfy all my cravings. I know I have to let go of everything that has control over me so I can give God full control of my life.

Jeanine

Summers were my favorite as a child. I remember waking up early and going to my grandparent's house for breakfast, then we would go swimming in their backyard. We arrived at my favorite place on the planet, where we would sit down to a full breakfast of bacon, eggs, sausage, hash browns, and sometimes pancakes. I got to sit next to the man I loved most in the world and listen to him tell stories. I remember him looking down and over at me with nothing but love and giving me more bacon off his plate. Then he would kick us kids out to the backyard to swim. He always worked in the garden while watching us. During breaks from swimming, we picked tomatoes and lemons from the yard and ran to the huge freezer on the porch to get ice cream. Then we were called in for lunch, and it started all over. This was my happy place, surrounded by food and love.

When my grandpa got sick and the breakfasts stopped, I still looked for comfort and love from food. I became a fat child and got bullied and teased endlessly for it, but I just couldn't stop eating. I couldn't stop looking for that comfort I missed so much. But that all changed when my mom decided to send me to a summer camp. You don't get to eat whatever you want to when you are at summer camp. I only got to eat at mealtime and one snack a day. That summer, I finally lost weight. I had to get all new clothes for school. I remember being elated when I actually got to buy teen sizes and not adult. For the first time in years, I was excited to start school. That was when I found my new comfort. That hole inside of me, that grief, was not being filled up by food anymore, but by attention. I had found my new addiction.

I knew I wasn't the prettiest girl and that I was weird. I had too many opinions and liked to talk about nerdy, uncool things. However, I realized that if I could be skinny, if I could wear cool clothes, if I made myself into what people thought I should be, I could be accepted. I started dieting, restricting my calories, and being conscious of what I said and how I looked.

I started riding horses and training, which only helped me lose more weight and get more attention. I loved it. People were being nice to me, and boys were actually talking to me. What more could a teenage girl want? I wanted more of it. But the hole inside me—the grief and depression—was still there. When I looked in the mirror, I still saw a fat girl. It didn't matter what the scale said. The attention I got wasn't enough. That's when I felt like I'd lost control.

I refused to go back to being overweight, so I started controlling how much food came into my body. I felt peaceful for the first time in years, and I couldn't get enough. My horseback riding trainer noticed my lack of strength and stamina and kept making comments. Then one day my horse slipped because I couldn't support him on a landing. I was so afraid that I'd hurt him that I started eating normally again. That saved me from full-blown anorexia.

I struggled again during pregnancy. But when my precious baby girl was born, nothing else mattered. My entire perspective on self-worth changed.

But even now, when life gets stressful, I catch myself limiting my food intake. Now I can stop myself before it gets out of hand. I know that God created us all in our own perfectly imperfect ways. I want my daughter to love and treat her body with respect just the way it is, because it is perfect. So when I am faced with an insecure day, I ask myself, "Would you want your daughter to think this way?"

It's My Signature Sin
DAYS 37–40

Come and hear, all you who fear God; let me tell you what he had done for me. I cried out to him with my mouth; his praise was on my tongue. If I had cherished sin in my heart, the Lord would not have listened; but God has surely listened and has heard my prayer. Praise be to God, who has not rejected my prayer or withheld his love from me!

Psalm 66:16–20

When I saw Dr. Michael Mangis's book *Signature Sins: Taming Our Wayward Hearts* online, I immediately stopped and read the summary. The author set out to equip believers to honestly delve into the root of their most private sins so they could stop trying to hide them and experience true freedom in Christ.

I first heard the term *signature sin* when our young family started attending a church in Northern California. One Sunday, the pastor preached a sermon on the topic. He informed the congregation that each of us had a personal area of sin that we repeatedly struggled with and tried to hide. According to the pastor, this signature sin was different for every person. For one it might be abusing alcohol, for another lust, for another compulsive eating, and someone else might resist giving back to God through tithes. When he asked everyone to pray and ponder, seek God, and earnestly petition Him to reveal our signature sin, I brushed it off as an issue that didn't apply to me. I was a good Christian, a devoted wife, an attentive mother, a committed servant in ministries. I didn't drink to excess, lie, cheat, or steal, and I'd never committed adultery. This was for other people in church, the *real* sinners, those who were babes in the Lord, not me. When the service ended, I left the sanctuary in blissful denial and went on with my day.

But my pastor's words kept coming back to me. *Each of us has a signature sin. What is yours?* If we all had one, didn't *all* include me? I knew the Bible verse that mentioned "the sin that so easily entangles" (Hebrews 12:1). Was that another way of referring to a signature sin? But I honestly couldn't think of anything in my life that was that bad.

The topic came up again while I was talking to a work associate, Bob, who happened to also be a pastor. He finally explained the concept to me in a way that I could understand.

Bob placed his hands flat on the work counter and spread them about twelve inches apart. "See this gap between my hands?"

"Yes."

"Think of the gap as your Christian walk. One hand is you, the other is Jesus. As you move closer to Jesus, He reveals stuff along the way, including areas of sin. When you deal with those things, the gap gets smaller."

He moved his hands closer together.

Ah, I thought. The gap was like the barnacle analogy I often used, comparing myself to the bottom of a ship with barnacles all over it that are hidden from the surface. I think my skin is soft and smooth until I plunge below the surface, God points out the barnacles, and I look at them. *Eww! How long has* that *been an issue?* If I want to get rid of it, I must acknowledge what God has revealed and scrape it off. Then I see another one and deal it, then another one, until those nasty, crusty, almost impenetrable parasites are gone. Each time I do this, I grow closer to Jesus as I approach Him with a purer heart. Those problem areas are almost always areas of sin.

So I did have sin. *God, I am truly sorry. How could I be so arrogant to assume that a sermon about sin applied to everyone else in the room except me?*

But what was my signature sin?

Before writing this study, I had put myself in the trenches of surrender. I devoted forty days to the process, spent time in prayer, fasted, studied the Bible, and gave God free rein over my heart. I found that He totally astonished me by faithfully revealing each area of control and weakness that I prayed for. He showed me how to press in and recognize areas where I had more than a few barnacles. In other words, I had allowed Him to identify my sins. So if I had sins like everyone else, I had a signature sin like everyone else too.

I walked away from the conversation with Bob humbled. It was time to do what my pastor had encouraged and ask God to reveal the thing that repeatedly reared its ugly head.

One day while riding in the car with my husband, I started praying silently, asking God to please show me my signature sin. *Reveal it to me, Lord. I am ready to acknowledge it and let you start weeding it out of my life.*

Later, while cleaning my bedroom, I found myself tiding up after my husband and getting annoyed. Why wasn't he tidier? I started thinking about our similarities and differences and finally figured out the problem behind the messy bedroom: *I'm a doer and he isn't. This mess is an example of that.*

That was when it hit me. *Wham!* I had unearthed my hidden signature sin. It was my terrible tendency to be critical and judgmental. If someone isn't like me, I start judging and labeling them. Instead of seeing the beauty in how God made them and learning to love them for the gifts that He gave them, I come down hard and see the parts of them that bug me. I'm quick to make assumptions based on my version of the story. Instead of focusing on the hard work my husband does to provide for his family, I see his clutter in the bedroom or an unfinished project and decide, *He's not a doer like perfect me.*

I do it with people outside my family too, including people I've never met. If a lady at church is quiet, I label her stuck up. If someone is having difficulties with her teenager or in her marriage, I assume she must be doing something wrong. If I see a child throwing a fit in the store, I judge the mom. *My kids would* never *do that. Because they would know better!*

This is absolutely, without a doubt, my signature sin. I never called it sin until that day. I called it being opinionated, observant, intuitive, or unafraid to speak my mind. But what does God's Word say in Matthew 7:1–2? "Do not judge, or you too will be judged. For in the same way you judge others, you will be judged, and with the measure you use, it will be measured to you."

And then there's that passage about ignoring the log in my own eye while pointing out the fleck in someone else's.

I think the Bible would call my log a critical spirit.

It was time to name it, confess it, and let God work on me.

Lord, forgive me for having a critical spirit, I prayed. *Help me to see the good in people instead of what I consider a weakness.*

Just as Bob said that day in the work room, allowing God to bring my signature sin to light drew me closer to Him. I no longer needed to hide behind my excuses. The barnacles were coming off.

Jesus came to free us from our sin—to stand next to the judgment throne of God the Father and say, "Your sin is forgiven." This includes those sins that so easily beset us.

What would you say is your signature sin? Like me, do you tend to be critical? Are you quick tempered or prone to gossip? Maybe you struggle with an addiction and fear reaching out for help and being judged. Or maybe, like me, you're still waiting for God to make your signature sin clear to you. Whatever it is, know that His grace extends to all our sins, including the ones we try to hide or are blind to. As you allow God access to the darkest corners of your heart, ask Him to allow you to feel the freedom that comes with bringing it into the light.

Day 37: Pray for ten minutes without interruption

Lord, today I invite You to show me my signature sin. Remove the scales from my eyes. Open my heart and my mind, dear Lord. Show Your daughter those things that only You can allow me to see. My precious Father, I love you. I want to grow ever closer to You. When I move from this life to the next, I want You to see me as a woman who lived to please You. Lord, I thank You for providing me with answers when I earnestly seek You with all my heart. Thank You for Your forgiveness and grace. Amen and Amen!

Write down what God reveals to you as you pray.
- _____
- _____
- _____

Day 38: Fast/Sacrifice for twenty-four hours
Write down what God reveals to you during the fast.
- _____
- _____
- _____

Day 39: Identify
Write down the secret sin that you have identified.
- _____
- _____
- _____

Day 40: Take action
What do you plan to do differently now that you know your areas of weakness?
- _____
- _____
- _____

It's My Signature Sin: Other Women's Stories

Melissa

Ouch! When I asked God to reveal my signature sin, He helped me see two. The first is my tendency to be ungrateful. He even challenged me to go back to the previous chapter in this book and be grateful for the body He blessed me with. It's time for me to see it as a gift from Him.

Next, He revealed my sin of negativity. I now understand that this damages me and hurts others. It is also an insult to God, who has given me so many good things.

I hate my sin of negativity. (See, even now I'm being negative by using the word *hate*.) It darkens my mind. It causes me to grumble and complain. One daughter calls me Eeyore when I get on a negativity rant. Even small bumps in the road of life can trigger negativity, especially when they get added to a few other small bumps. My negative attitude is usually connected to fear. Thus, it reflects a lack of trust in God and His power to protect, provide, and care for all that concerns me.

I've prayed often for my mind to be transformed and for God to help me take every thought captive in obedience to Christ. This dark, critical thinking is like a blight on my mind, sometimes making me physically or emotionally crippled.

The fears behind these areas of weakness go way back. When I was nine, my mom suffered a nervous breakdown. She was hospitalized for a month or more, but to me it felt like forever. In her eyes this was an enormous stigma. We were forbidden to tell anyone about her mental struggles. I could not tell anyone why my mom was in the hospital. We kids were told that we had to behave, or mom might have to go away again. None of us had caused Mom's illness, but we were held to an impossible standard anyway. I began to fear that I would end up like her. I have prayed against it all of my life.

Fortunately, by His grace, God revealed Himself to me in a personal way when I was in my thirties. My mother never experienced that. I can bring my dark thoughts and the shadows of my sinful thinking to God and allow Him and the truths of His Word to show me I am loved and accepted, and even a delight to Him. His Spirit transforms my thinking and helps me capture those wrong thoughts. It is a battle I fight daily. Each morning I have a routine of putting on the full armor of God. Without Him I would live in a deep, dark pit of despair. I am grateful to have a divine Counselor.

Now that He has gently revealed the truth, my heavenly Father can help me turn my negative thoughts around to praises, thankfulness, and how I might bless others.

Kathi

I had to pray very hard while asking God what it was that made me stumble. In the past, I drank and did drugs to escape. I became very promiscuous after I was raped. Now that I've become sober, I often overeat to cover my feelings and my frustrations. I also isolate myself.

I've had to search the Bible to find out which of those actions were really sin. Overeating and isolation sneak up on me. Most of the time I don't even realize I'm doing it. But now I know. God helped me recognize that my signature sin is laziness.

"Lazy hands make for poverty, but diligent hands bring wealth," Proverbs 10:14 says.

Proverbs 12:24 reminds me, "Diligent hands will rule, but laziness ends in forced labor."

When I overeat or hibernate instead of deal with the problem that is causing me to do those things, I'm taking the easy way out. I'm being lazy.

God is wonderful in His ways of revealing the truth. I was lazy when I drank and did drugs. It was a pattern I'd carried through my entire life. If something got too hard, I gave up and took the consequences. It was easier to accept things as they were than it was to do the work required for a better outcome, especially if I didn't know if my hard work would pay off. It was very hard to do things the right way and to ask for God's help when I didn't know what to do next.

Soon after I was baptized in water, I decided to let God help me live in a way that pleased Him. He started showing me that I could do anything with His strength. I could even turn my life around for the better. Now I'm like a child discovering a new world: God's world. It makes me giggle and cry all at the same time. I am conquering more new tasks all the time. But I'm learning to ask for His help and guidance, which is also hard. I want to be independent, but God wants us to live and love and help each other go through this life. I'm also learning that when I ask for help, God's answer often includes me needing to do something—that He doesn't just drop what I need into my lap. I need to learn to do what makes me feel uncomfortable once in a while.

I am happy that God has revealed this hidden sin to me. Now that I am aware of it, I will be less apt to stumble into the same old pattern of laziness. When I catch myself reaching for food instead of dealing with what is upsetting me or isolating instead of doing what needs to be done, I can call on the power of Jesus, and His grace will pull me forward to new accomplishments. I truly believe the verse in Scripture that says anyone who belongs to Christ has become a new person. The old life is gone, a new life has begun! Second Corinthians 5:17 can now be my life verse. Christ is the center of it all, including my new life.

Shelley

My signature sin is being critical in my thinking and what I say about others. It's hard to admit, but it's true.

While exercising to a Zumba high-energy video, I suddenly pictured a rusty, dirt-caked oil container with a spout. That was me and my heart before this study. Is an oil tin useful? Yes. It can be extremely helpful for certain things. But who wanted oil spilled all over them, especially when they didn't ask for any?

Then a new picture came to mind, of a crystal-clear glass beaker (the kind we use in chem lab). It was transparent and filled with fresh, clean water. That was what I wanted my heart to look like: pure, inviting, and ready to quench (not drown) those who feel parched.

I prayed Psalm 51:10: "Create in me a clean heart, O God, and renew a right spirit within me."

Then I prayed Jeremiah 12:3: "But as for me, LORD, you know my heart. You see me and test my thoughts."

Psalm 26:2 reminded me, "Put me on trial, LORD, and cross-examine me. Test my motives and my heart."

In Psalm 24:4 I read, "The one who has clean hands and a pure heart, who has not set his mind on what is false."

When I let God examine my heart, I saw that it was putrid on the inside. Now it is becoming clean.

It's not always pretty, but it's a start.

I can't help thinking of a time when I was in junior high, rail thin, flat as a pancake, with a pixie haircut, ugly glasses, and braces complete with a head gear. Like every other girl my age, I was seriously under construction. At that time, I was living under the shadow of my sister Robin, who was two years older and seemed light years ahead of me.

One day, as I strolled into the lunchroom clutching my brown paper lunch bag, the most popular girl at school swung her arm across my shoulders and started talking to me. It didn't last long, but as she patted me on the back and walked away, I hoped the other kids saw me with her. For the rest of the afternoon I floated through the halls and my classes hoping that maybe I could now be part of the "in" group.

During my last class of the day, I leaned back and heard a crinkling sound. I reached over my shoulder and discovered a piece of paper stuck to my sweater. In huge green letters it said, *If you think the back of me looks bad, just look at the front!* Yes, I had worn that piece of paper for hours and no one had said a word. After a long bus ride home, I wept in my room alone, telling no one.

Events like this and other humiliations, such as failing my nursing boards after five years of college, seared through my heart like fire. I slowly turned bitter and negative. But now I understand that those experiences also made me empathetic. When asked to lead a devotion for eighth graders, I shared my story about the note on my back. You could hear a pin drop—not because of me, but because God had stirred their hearts. It reminded me that He is now turning my most painful moments into opportunities. So why be bitter about anything that God might eventually use for good?

Conclusion: Celebrating the Journey

What a difference forty days makes! After spending almost six weeks in complete surrender to God, remaining committed to prayer, fasting, identifying what God put on my heart, and taking steps toward change, I felt like a different woman. Not only had God answered my prayer to know Him more and revealed the rewards of giving everything to Him, but my gracious heavenly Father had also shown me the blessings in allowing Him to reveal the core of what held me back from the closeness I craved: my sins.

But what surprised me most during my 40 Days of Surrender was the way God used this process and the book that it inspired to reach and touch other women. It was a remarkable privilege to witness God's transforming work in their lives as they bravely embraced the process of surrendering all to Him.

Just as He had done with me, the Lord gently identified the small pebbles that, over the journey of their lives, had become repetitive stumbling blocks for them. Together we discovered that those rocks on our paths created barriers and dividers in our relationships with others, in our relationship with God, and in our faith. We found that surrender truly was the key to unlocking the door to a fulfilled life where we could freely use our gifts, let God heal deep wounds, and live with confidence as the person God created us to be. Ultimately, we learned that God does not demand that we surrender so He can take more from us, He lovingly calls us to surrender so He can give us more of what we need most: Him.

I hope that by reading this book and taking your own journey of surrender, you have experienced new freedom as well. I pray that you will continue to grow closer to the Lord and experience the joy and blessing of giving Him everything. In those moments when you feel like you've slipped back into old patterns (because we all do occasionally), remember that we are all on a path of continual growth. All you have to do is run to the One who knows and loves you most and surrender again.

About the Author

Jeanette M. Towne is the former President and CEO of a U. S. based technology Corporation. Her one-man, start-up company evolved into a thriving, multi-million-dollar enterprise and in 2020 her corporation was acquired by a global enterprise technology partner. With a goal of helping to introduce God to others, in 2022, Jeanette became the CEO and co-founder of Stone Impact Media, an inspirational streaming film and production corporation. Jeanette is the published author of her true story, Lifted From Darkness, and has completed a screenplay based on the miraculous journey. She and her husband Sam have been married for over 30-years, sharing life with their four adult children, 3 'In-Loves', 3 perfect grandsons, while navigating an empty nest with a growing family of 12, now spread out in four states! Jeanette is passionate about sharing her incredible message, and has been featured on many Christian TV and radio programs, such as; The 700 Club, CHVN – The Morning Show, Woman to Woman, and a 2-week segment featured on "Unshackled!". She is an engaging, transparent and inspirational communicator, and has spoken at many community, business and women's events. She was a featured author, Women of Faith Conference in Austin, Texas.

    Jeanette devotes time to family and friends, spiritual mentoring, couples mentoring, and playing keyboard in her church worship team. She, along with four other Women of Faith speakers, created and launched Uncensored Hearts in 2017 (www.uncensoredhearts.org). Their goal is to open women up to slices of real life that don't look "clean" in the eyes of the church. Uncensored Hearts ministers to believers and strives to reach nonbelievers for Christ as well.

As a survivor of domestic violence who almost became a murder victim, Jeanette strongly feels that she owes each breath to her God. This passion compels her to help inform, educate, and inspire women to freedom.

Jeanette's life verse is Psalm 40:1–2:

> *I waited patiently for the Lord;*
> *he turned to me and heard my*
> *cry. He lifted me out of the slimy*
> *pit, out of the mud and mire;*
> *he set my feet on a rock*
> *and gave me a firm place to stand.*

Order Information

To order additional copies of this book, please visit
www.redemption-press.com.
Also available on Amazon.com and BarnesandNoble.com
or by calling toll-free 1-844-2REDEEM.

CPSIA information can be obtained
at www.ICGtesting.com
Printed in the USA
BVHW081800200322
631576BV00003B/16